· THE FATHERLESS FATHER ·

To Chad,

You are always one thought away
from starting the journey to
achieving what you desire! I wish
you all the success that you
deserve! God Bless!

Best, Recr Y. M...

▪ THE FATHERLESS FATHER ▪

*HOW A SINGLE MOTHER'S STRENGTH
TURNED A BOY INTO A MAN*

By Reco McDaniel

www.TheFatherlessFather.com

The Fatherless Father
Copyright © 2012, by Reco McDaniel

Contact Us:
2385 Wall Street
Conyers, GA 30013
office: 1.800.995.5251   fax: 678.528.9513
email: info@thefatherlessfather.com
web: www.thefatherlessfather.com

ISBN 978-0-9887342-0-3

This book is available at quantity discounts for bulk purchase.

Printed in the United States of America

"What happens to us does not determine where we end up in life. It's how we react to what happens to us. That will determine our future."

-Reco McDaniel

Family
God's Greatest Gift

Thank you Shanee', Reco Jr., and
Raegan for supporting and loving
me through it all.
I love you!

Table of Contents

Dedication

July 21, 1962 – July 31, 2011

I would like to dedicate this book to the only father
I knew for the first 30 years of my life – my mother,
Deborah Ann Watson.

If I could define strength, tenacity, independence,
determination, hardworking, persistence, and
resolve in one word it would be simply – Momma. I
owe mostly everything I know and my life today to
you! I love you!

Until we meet again...

Momma's foundation to her strength

Footprints in the Sand

One night I dreamed I was walking along the beach
with the Lord.

Many scenes from my life flashed across the sky.

In each scene I noticed footprints in the sand.

Sometimes there were two sets of footprints, other
times there were one set of footprints.

This bothered me because I noticed that during the
low periods of my life,

when I was suffering from anguish, sorrow or
defeat,

I could see only one set of footprints.

So I said to the Lord,

"You promised me Lord, that if I followed you, you
would walk with me always.

But I have noticed that during the most trying
periods of my life there have only been one set of
footprints in the sand.

Why, when I needed you most, you have not been
there for me?"

The Lord replied,

"The times when you have seen only one set of
footprints

is when I carried you."

-Author Unknown

Intro

"A man can be as great as he wants to be. If you believe in yourself and have the courage, the determination, the dedication, the competitive drive, and if you are willing to sacrifice the little things in life and pay the price for the things that are worthwhile, it can be done."

–Vince Lombardi, Legendary Football Coach

When I first set out to write this book, I wanted to create a simple tale about my life—a way for people to know about my trials and tribulations, how I overcame certain challenges in my life, and how these tests turned me into the man I am today. By doing so, I figured this would allow the reader to gain a better understanding of my upbringing, which, ultimately, would inspire them to live a better life.

However, I soon began to realize that this book needed more substance than that. It needed to allow the reader to *truly* understand that *their* struggles were once *my own* and that it *is* possible to overcome their issues. There are many people walking around the world at this very moment who feel like they're alone... that their life obstacles are shared with no one else. This creates a sense of loneliness with countless people around the world. Just think about it. How many people do you know that are struggling to make ends meet? How many single mothers do you know who are working three jobs, barely keeping enough food on the table for her family, and genuinely trying to ensure that her children are cared for, even though it seems like an impossible task as she drags herself out of bed at 5 a.m. every morning? I'm sure you know a child who is angry at the world because he or she feels as though no one understands what they're feeling on the inside and how their resentment is caused by feelings of neglect or not obtaining enough love from their parents. We all know these stories. I wanted to make it my mission to help address them through my story.

I travel around the country meeting thousands of people each year, many of whom ask me "How can I live a better life?" or "How were you able to operate at the level you're at right now when the beginning of your life didn't seem so promising?" I often have to take a step back and really think about how my story can help alter the way one sees their circumstances, which, in the end, can help change the way they see themselves and the world around them. The conclusion I've come to is this: We all have different stories that start off differently and will end differently. However, there are similarities and shared experiences that we can piece together with one another, mainly to show we are going through the same tests, and we can learn through one another, especially if it can help the end result be positive.

In the end, I hope this book inspires young mothers, young fathers, single parents, teenage boys, runaways, fatherless fathers, and a multitude of other groups to understand that just because your story started out rough, it doesn't mean it will end that way. I have faith that it will allow you to see that the world holds many positive experiences and possibilities for you, but you won't ever be able to see them unless you've got the right mindset, the will to work hard, and the passion to follow your dreams.

The following pages will give you frank and upfront recollections of my past, my present, and my future. My past allowed me to appreciate my present life. My present life allows me to have hope for myself, my family, and for future generations. I am optimistic this hope will inspire the same in you.

Chapter 1 – Feelings of the Fatherless

"You might be locked in a world not of your own making, her eyes said, but you still have a claim on how it is shaped. You still have responsibilities."
–Barack Obama, *Dreams from My Father: A Story of Race and Inheritance*

Picture this: A 6'1" black man sprinting like he's in the 100-meter dash in the Olympics through Orlando International Airport after a long, tiresome day but still needing to catch a 1:15 p.m. flight back to Atlanta, Georgia. This is me on a muggy July day in Florida. I'm blowing past security, dodging my way around other wayward passengers, trying to make that flight. Yes—suit, tie, and all. My heart's racing as my mind is replaying the highlights of my life-changing weekend I just experienced at the National Speakers Association National Convention. Suddenly, between hearing "Just the Way You Are" by Bruno

Mars over the airport's loudspeaker for what seems to be the tenth time on this trip, I hear an automated voice say, "The tram is now departing." I quickly make a promise to myself that it will *not* be leaving without me—I've got to get home.

I manage to squeeze through the 12-inch opening in the tram doors as they quickly shut behind me. The other passengers in the tram car briefly look my way, mainly to make sure I made it on in one piece, because they have been in my position before—running through the airport as if it's a scene from *Home Alone*. I look down at my watch and see that it is 1:00 p.m. I begin to have a minor panic attack because my flight will depart soon. Fifteen minutes and counting. I think, *How did I let time get away from me so badly that I'm rushing through the airport? I can't do this again—this is crazy.* I begin racing down the escalator at full speed, like a running back going in for the game-winning touchdown, brushing past families, businessmen, and everyone in between, quickly apologizing for all the commotion. But again, they don't look too irritated because it seems they can empathize with my situation. At this point, there is only one thing on my mind: my son. I cannot miss this flight. I will not break my promise. I will be at his football game tonight, and I will give him our ritual pre-game pep talk.

I look up at the terminal clock, and it says 1:07 p.m. I'm sweating profusely from all the running, and the perspiration begins to drip down my face. The suit I have on doesn't make it any better, but it was a necessity for the conference. I can still hear my mother's voice telling me to "always look my best." This, however, happens to be one of those times that I wish I had on a comfortable t-shirt with some basketball shorts and running shoes.

Finally, I look up and see I'm at Terminal B. I just need to run past 10 gates, and I'm on the next flight to see my boy. I grin with thoughts of witnessing his smile light up when he sees me and keep it as I move through the airport. Through the blur of faces, baby cries, and endless food vendors creeps Gate 85. I slow down with a sigh of relief and thank God that I've made it before they closed the cabin doors. I don't know what I would have done if I ran all this way just to see the door close in my face. "Well, you just made it with 4 minutes to spare! Hurry on now, ya hear," shouts a sweet old southern accent from the check-in counter. As I approach the boarding door, I am met with reassuring brown eyes and a smile by the woman collecting the tickets. It's as though she can feel how hard I worked to get to the gate. "It's alright now, you've made it," she quietly tells me. I catch my breath, quickly hand over my ticket, and rush on the plane with my heart pounding and sweat dripping all over, yet grinning ear to ear because I'm ready to see my son.

I take my seat, ready for the plane to take off as soon as possible. Suddenly, the flight attendant appears.

"Would you like a cold bottle of water, sir?" she says.

"How could you tell? Am I sweating that much?" I reply with a smile on my face.

"Yes, sir. We don't usually pass out drinks before the plane takes off, but I think we can make an exception for you. You seem like you need it," she says, nods, and kindly walks away.

I smirk and gratefully take the bottle of water. I'm sure people around me are a little jealous at the special treatment I just received, but I ignore it. Seeing my son's face will make this entire adventure worth it.

As I get comfortable in my snug airplane seat, my adrenaline is still rushing through my veins. I figured that because I'll have downtime for the next hour, I will download all of the excitement of the last few days. During that time, I met some of the most successful speakers, authors, and motivators from around the world.

> **"In the midst of all the successful individuals, I stopped and realized how blessed I was to have reached such high peaks of success at my early age—I have much more than I could have ever dreamed of as a kid."**

There were men and women representing various ethnic, religious, and culture backgrounds from San Diego, California to London, England and New York, New York to San Juan, Puerto Rico. Everyone was out in full force, allowing themselves to learn from other successful motivators while appreciating the moment—rubbing elbows with the world's greats was exciting for everyone in attendance.

In the midst of all the successful individuals, I stopped and realized how blessed I was to have reached such high peaks of success at my early age—I have much more than I could have ever dreamed of as a kid. When I was a child growing up in the 1980s, I stood around wondering where my father was while admiring my mother's hard work from afar. I struggled with feelings of inadequacy, hoping that, one day, I would be able to take a life that started in the projects and do something amazing and influential with it.

And here I was.

I became a multi-million dollar producing entrepreneur within the network marketing industry in my mid-20s, having addressed tens of thousands across the country through motivation and training. In addition to this, I've received numerous awards and recognition. I've built a gratifying lifestyle, one where I don't have to worry about my lights being turned off or not having enough gas in my car to get me to a destination. I've surrounded myself with mentally strong and hardworking people, and we feed off of each other's good vibes and push each other to work harder, faster, and more efficiently. I've had the opportunity to travel the world: I've marveled at the Christ the Redeemer statue in Rio de Janeiro, Brazil in one moment and visited Buckingham Palace and Big Ben in London in the next. I was blessed to meet the woman of my dreams, Shanee', and have her accept me as her husband—one of the greatest gifts any person could have ever given me. Additionally, I have two amazing children who are everything I could have ever dreamed them to be, who make me laugh until my sides hurt, and who also remind me how much of an influence I have in their lives as their father. Last, but certainly not least, I have God, who has brought me through so many trials and tribulations. It's hard not to think of Psalm 34:4, which says, "I sought the LORD, and He heard me, and delivered me from all my fears."

And yet, despite all these wonderful things, I know my purpose is greater. I know there is more work for me to do.

"God has been so good to me," I quietly mumble to myself with a smile.

As I continue to reflect on my life, I hear a young child behind me begin to speak.

"Mommy, how come I never see my dad?" I hear the little boy ask his mother.

This innocent question completely diminishes all thoughts in my head, and I begin to listen intently for the response. As I wait for the answer, I hear a painfully familiar pause of silence as the mother wraps her arms around her son and explains, "It's me, you, and God, and we are incredibly blessed, don't you think?"

I can tell he has dropped his head as he solemnly replies, "Yes mommy, we are blessed."

At this moment, my heart pains for this young boy, and I am struck with a series of emotions, as if I am that boy again; bitterness, sadness, emptiness, and jealousy quickly begin to sneak into my heart. These old emotions I thought I had put to rest rear their ugly heads, reminding me that I never quite got over my experiences as a child. I think about the fact that I never had a father growing up and how that shaped me to be the man I am today, whether those moments were good, bad, or ugly. However, I begin to think about the countless conversations I had with my own mother, and I smile. I feel joy in my heart in that moment, realizing how amazing that woman was—simply recalling how through it all, she was my saving grace.

While the mother and son behind me are having a bonding moment, I realize how strong my own mother was and how much I loved and appreciated her for raising me the way she did. I think about how much I love God for providing me with such a close-knit family, even though my biological father, my blood, was not in the home with me. My thoughts drift again to the two behind me, specifically to the little boy, who can only be about 8 years old, and how there are countless other young males out there with no father to look up to or who would be there to encourage, support, and guide them. They also wonder where their fathers are when it's time to play catch, when they score their first touchdown, and when they get their acceptance letters into college. They wonder if they did something wrong to "push" their fathers away, hoping that, one day, he will walk through the front door with arms wide open and say three simple words, "I'm home, son."

I was quickly saddened, realizing the severity of this epidemic in today's society—how it's a social norm to be in a single-parent household with no father—and even sadder to realize that often times, these young boys don't have other family members to lean on, as I had. I begin to think about the fact that I am a father and how seriously I take my duty and responsibility; how I take every hurt growing up and make that a place of joy for my son. However, I also understand that this is often not the case for many young people in today's society—many parents take their hurt and inflict it on their children who are defenseless against their parent's wrath. What's even more unfortunate is how many men these days have children and then leave them fatherless, simply because they did not have a father in their home growing up—the wretched cycle continuing.

As the plane begins its ascent into the open summer sky on its way to Atlanta, I have a moment of revelation. I realize the next level of my purpose and the new chapter in my story: writing a book that will help address the internal conflicts that numerous people are dealing with on a daily basis. In this moment, I realized that it was now part of my mission to help address the emotions surrounding people who are without a husband, a mentor, a partner, or a father who is willing to step in and help take care of his family. Those thoughts helped to set the foundation of this book. The words on these pages will help encourage, inspire, motivate, and bring awareness to men, women, and children who are currently experiencing or have experienced single parenthood.

I want this book to help those growing up without a father. I want it to touch those developing into manhood without a male influence. I want it to assist men who never knew their father but are not using that as an excuse to be absent from their children's lives. Hopefully, fathers struggling to provide consistent attention to their children will gain some inspiration from my words. This book will provide simple success principles about life that will leave people feeling more confident about themselves, their specific life situation, and their relationships with their family. My mission, with the assistance of this book, is to lay out applicable steps to free people from any stronghold related to this growing epidemic of single-parent households and help them begin living lives without limits and walk into their true and provisioned destiny.

> **"I am proof that although your beginning may not start out as you dreamed it to be, that does not mean your future can't be something wonderful."**

I don't claim to be a licensed counselor, family therapist, or holder of a PhD who has conducted in-depth research on the causes and effects of single-parent households in a greater society and what this potentially means for the future of the world. I have not conducted hundreds of interviews with young men, asking them their thoughts on growing up with a dad in their lives and what that does for their self-esteem and their self-worth. Additionally, I don't have any concrete evidence on whether or not young men who are raised by a single mother have a greater likelihood of getting into trouble with the law, which ultimately leads to a life behind bars. *However*, I AM a man who experienced life without a father, overcame all of the adversity associated with being without an *active* male parental figure, reached numerous peaks of success, and became a reliable and dedicated father to my two children. I am proof that although your beginning may not start out as you dreamed it to be, that does not mean your future can't be something wonderful.

I am a Fatherless Father.

The Fatherless Father

Chapter 2 – Faith and the Will to Live

"He said to them, 'Because of your little faith. For truly, I say to you, if you have faith like a grain of mustard seed, you will say to this mountain, 'Move from here to there,' and it will move, and nothing will be impossible for you.'" –Matthew 17:20

Weeks had passed since the conference, and I was beginning to feel very overwhelmed. Monday was running into Tuesday and Tuesday into Wednesday. Each day became a blur, and the stresses of life were compounding on my shoulders. At the time, I was in the midst of an ugly legal battle that was taking a toll on my professional life, as well as my personal life. Furthermore, I had just created a new company, my wife had recently become pregnant, I was actively engaged in the motivational speaking world, and, to top it off, I just found out life-altering news: My mother was diagnosed with cancer. It was almost as if I was drowning in life's surprises. Despite these things, there was this persistent need to place my words to others down in a book; the burning responsibility to write these pages somehow always stayed at the forefront of my mind.

My world seemed to be caving in; there was so much joy yet so much sorrow all at once. To be honest, I was stretching myself trying to find a way to stay positive, searching my spirit for inspiration. I kept thinking to myself, *I must keep myself going for my family, for my business, for myself.* In those moments, I remembered the story my grandmother always told about how strong my mother was right around the time of my birth. The circumstances that surrounded my birth—and the months and years that followed that date—helped to test the true character of my mother, something I referred to during this time in my life. I thought, *If Momma could hold it down with far less than I have now, surely I can press on.* She was that kind of woman: the type of individual that left one inspired, even when she wasn't around to have her presence felt.

Chapter 2 – Faith and the Will to Live

Now, when I was born, there weren't any photos taken of me. There wasn't one taken of my mother holding me moments after she had given birth. There weren't any cute pictures of me sleeping in the baby nursery with a dozen other children who were brought into the world on that day. No photos were taken of me during my first feeding, my first sleep, or even my first diaper change.

There was nothing.

It may be hard for some to believe, but there were no pictures of me until I was about 5 or 6 months old. You may wonder why this rite of passage did not happen.

The answer is quite simple: The doctors told my mother and grandmother that I was not going to live.

My premature birth came around the end of my mother's second trimester. Here I was, coming into the world at the end of the sixth month of her pregnancy. As you can imagine, this was an alarming experience for my small immediate family. I was born at 2lbs 2oz. Take a moment to let that marinate in your mind. I weighed less than a telephone book, a bag of sugar, or a laptop computer—everyday items that people pick up without much effort. It's important to note that babies typically lose weight right after birth before they gain weight, so at one point I went down to 1lb 2oz. It is honestly a blessing from God that I was even able to survive such an improbable hardship as that one. When I reflect back on this time in my life, I realize that I've always been destined to overcome obstacles, no matter how daunting they may seem at the time.

My grandmother would later tell me she tried to get my mom to avoid seeing me so much while I was in the incubator. She was afraid my mom would become too attached to me when they all thought it was a matter of time before I passed away. In hindsight, I really can't blame this mentality. Honestly, what's the likelihood of a child with a dangerously low birth weight making it out of infancy without birth defects and lifelong disabilities that would have them sidelined their entire life?

My mom refused to give up on me and said no matter what, she would come every day after work and pray for me. And that's exactly what she did—she kept the faith. And slowly, without much fanfare, both my mother and grandmother would come pray for me each and every day. They would tell the doctor that no matter what he said, I was coming out of this. Simply put, they were speaking my little life into existence. It was a routine they followed: They lived their lives, took care of their outside obligations and tasks, and kept me prayed up. They would not be deterred from this path.

A period of time had passed, and the doctor said I was progressing; however, he said because I was so small, my lungs would never work properly, predicting major breathing ailments associated with underdeveloped lungs during the early moments of my life. It's important to note that my lungs had already collapsed twice before his prognosis. The doctor also told my mother and grandmother that I would never be a "normal" child and that I'd likely be a special needs child, would probably never speak, and in a worst-case scenario, I'd be a vegetable. My grandmother and mom refused to accept the doctor's diagnosis.

"Our God and your God must be two different higher powers because we don't accept this," they'd tell him. "Our child will make it through this. I don't care what your science says about him. God will bless him with the will to live, even if you won't."

A number of weeks had passed before they were allowed to bring me home. Days turned into weeks and weeks into months, and I was still alive and physically progressing at my own pace. My mother and grandmother said I didn't really talk during the first several months of my life. I also didn't seem to pay much attention to events going on around me. For example, people would talk and laugh around me, yet I wouldn't seem to react to them. Pots and pans would accidentally be dropped in the kitchen, and I would always look in the same direction, something that many would categorize as being odd. One day, when I was around 6 months old, the two women were sitting on the front porch of our home when a car drove up and honked the horn. Miraculously, I looked over in the direction of the car. At that moment, they both knew the doctor didn't know what he was talking about—I wasn't as bad off as he perceived me to be.

A few months later, my grandmother recalls my grandfather playing with me when she believes she heard me mumble something.

"You spoke, you made a sound, and you haven't shut up ever since," my grandmother would lovingly tell me as she recalled those first moments in my life.

She believed in me, my mother believed in me, and after those moments of hope, they were determined to keep their faith in God and me very strong.

> **"I was proof that faith 'as small as a mustard seed' was strong enough to keep me and my family moving forward...."**

As I started to get older, the doctor told my family that there was a slight chance that I would never walk. During that time, I would pull myself around instead of attempting to crawl like many babies tend to do during that stage in life. By 8 or 9 months old, I was still in the habit of pulling myself, and the doctors explained to my family that this was not normal or promising for my development. However, my mother and grandmother had witnessed other miracles during my short time on this earth, so they believed that things would get better for me. After another 4 to 5 months of this abnormal behavior, I was still scooting and pulling myself around. Finally, one day, I just got up and started walking. I never crawled as a baby; I just started walking! I was proof that faith "as small as a mustard seed" was strong enough to keep me and my family moving forward, only looking at the positive progress I had made. What was the point in focusing on my delayed development?

Years later, when I started school, the "experts" said I was not going to learn as fast as the other kids because they believed I was developmentally delayed. By the time I was in first grade, I was making straight A's. I later went on to graduate in the top of my class at my high school and was accepted into one of the top tech universities in the nation. They'd later go on to say that I would never be able to play sports like the rest of the kids because they predicted I would have asthma and other breathing issues. I played baseball from the age of 5 until I was in high school, along with football and basketball. Overall, these major life wins proved to me and all my naysayers at the time that I was mentally, physically, and emotionally strong enough to overcome statistical odds. My will and motivation were too strong to be torn down. I was on a mission to succeed, no matter how much outsiders doubted me.

When my grandmother and I recall this part of my life, I am immediately comforted knowing how much she and my mother were in my corner, allowing me to blossom far beyond my wildest dreams. I reflect on those formative years and remember that it doesn't matter what everyone out there says about you or what *they* believe you can achieve—the only thing that matters is what *you* believe. For me, my faith in God and my ability to press on through trying times is what got my family through my challenges.

Throughout my life, I remained centered with the Word of God and how He wanted me to live despite my circumstances. I won't lie, there were numerous times when I tried to challenge God. "Why must I always work harder than the other kids?" I would ask. "How many more obstacles do I need to face before I face no more?" I would wonder. Little did I know that countless other people ask these same questions when they're going through difficult times in their own lives.

I must admit, without having a father there to help me during these difficult moments in my life, I was secretly sad and bitter. I sometimes dreamed of having a father like other kids—a man that would stand by my side offering words of encouragement and teaching me how to dismiss the naysayers while becoming a man. I wanted a man there to tell me about the complexities surrounding girls and someone to tell me I was doing a great job in school, on the baseball field and basketball court, and in life. Although I knew I had the greatest Father of all, I still yearned to have my biological dad, my blood, to walk beside me on my journey. Regardless, I still had faith that things would work out for me and mostly kept these feelings to myself and told no one.

My mother and my grandmother modeled what it means to walk by faith not by sight. They taught me to believe in God always, knowing He will always provide. They showed me how I am a living testimony, even if my father was nowhere to be found. During my formative years, I had to have faith in myself, knowing that, one day, I would be great—so great that I'd be able to pass that knowledge on to others to show them their potential. With that being said, here are a few steps to help you keep your faith alive during challenging times:

1. **Always surround yourself with positive, forward thinking people.** There's nothing worse than allowing those with negative thoughts and beliefs to influence your mind and your life. Well-known actor Will Smith was quoted as saying, "You can tell how far in life you'll go by the five people you spend the most amount of time with." Just think of those words: the individuals you spend the most amount of time with will help dictate where your future goes. Isn't that powerful? Those who think positively will keep you uplifted, and you'll know they will always have your back— through the tough times when you want to give up and the good times when you're jumping up and down in

happiness. As media mogul Oprah Winfrey once said, "Lots of people want to ride with you in the limo, but what you want is someone who will take the bus with you when the limo breaks down." Do you know people like that?

2. **It's ok to get frustrated.** Nothing in this world is perfect. Not your financial situation, your home life, your responsibilities at work and school—nothing. It is actually a good thing to get frustrated with some of the circumstances we go through in life, whether we had a choice in something happening or we didn't. *However*, it is important to identify our frustrations and figure out ways to make them better. In short, use the frustration as your motivation to do something about it. For example, if you're getting poor grades in your English class, ask your teacher for help. Do not be ashamed. It's better to

ask for the help ahead of time instead of receiving the D in the class, correct? Life is all about acceptance or change. If you don't like something that is going on in your life, change it. If you can't change it, you must accept it and create a plan to deal with it as positively as possible. I've learned that it's not what happens to us in life that determines our results. What determines what we get in life is based on how we react to what happens to us. So, don't let your frustration make you bitter. Use it to make you better!

3. **See the end from the beginning.** Most of us get excited and inspired when we start something because we think of the end result, the goal. Typically, along the way to accomplishing that goal, whether it be trying to finish school, achieving success in business, or successfully raising our children, there are several tests we face that discourage us. The

tests are normally at the beginning and during the course of our journey. Most people focus on the tests, trials, and tribulations and forget about that goal or the end result they are looking for. Once this happens, you are in jeopardy of failing. You should always focus on the end result, not the trials that you may be presently faced with. If you focus on where you are, you will never be able to get where you're going.

4. **Pray.** This step is the easiest to do out of the four suggestions, but often times, it is the first one that is forgotten. Young people sometimes forget how powerful prayer can be in moments of happiness and times of despair. You can pray on the school bus, while you're paying your monthly bills, on the way to a job interview, before the big game with the cross-town rival, and even when you're sending in your college applications.

You can pray anytime, anywhere. It's important to remember that even the slaves back in the 1800s relied on prayer to help them through the daily beatings, inhumane living conditions, and the painfully aggressive workdays they were forced into. You should never be ashamed to pray, whether you believe in God the Father, Son, and Holy Spirit, Allah, Yahweh, Jehovah, or any other higher power. You should be able to create your very own personal relationship with that higher power, which will allow you to keep your faith strong. Do not rely on other people to create that bond for you. You must do it for yourself. There are a few Bible verses I look to in times of need.

- **Psalm 62:1**—My soul finds rest in God alone; my salvation comes from him.
- **Matthew 14:30**—LORD, save me.

- **Hebrews 11:1**—Now faith is being sure of what we hope for and certain of what we don't see.

- **1 Peter 5:9**—Resist him, standing firm in the faith, because you know that your brothers throughout the world are undergoing the same kind of sufferings.

- **2 Timothy 4:7**—I have fought the good fight, I have finished the race, I have kept the faith.

    You, of course, can look in the Bible for verses that connect with your life situation, but I'd suggest looking at Psalm and Proverbs for additional inspiration. I believe that once you read many of the lines in these books, your soul will find peace and your faith restored.

Anyone can tell that I had a slew of tests going on all at once at the beginning of my life. However, I found that all my burdens were lifted when I kept the faith. There was an overwhelming comfort that went on to follow me as an adult as I handled demanding situations with my business, my wife, my family, and my mother. To this day, I continue to smile at the adversity and remember at the end of the day that I have no choice but to take care of my responsibilities, raise my eyes to the sky, and thank God for giving me this life and allowing me to make the most of my trials each and every day.

The Fatherless Father

Chapter 3 – The Decision to Parent on Your Own

"God could not be everywhere and therefore he made mothers." —Jewish Proverb

There comes a time for many single mothers when they come to the realization that their child's father is never coming back. He won't be there to take his child to get ice cream, and he won't take them on carnival rides at the local fair. He won't scold them for climbing the tree on the playground, and he won't be there to comfort them when someone breaks their heart.

He will never show up.

In an ideal world, a mother would not have to raise her family on her own. This is the kind of place I wish for every person walking the planet—a place where the family unit works together as one, and a world where family disagreements between mothers and fathers are reconciled, everyone sits down together at dinner to talk about their days, and kids feel loved by both of their parents. However, this ideal world isn't the reality for a number of people. Some mothers are forced to raise their children on their own.

There are some of these fathers who do show up to help raise their children, but they're only there sporadically, never playing an *active* part in their children's lives. They may give money every so often or send a birthday card to their child when they remember, but they're never there like a father should be. It is unfortunate how many men don't understand how this type of behavior can be detrimental to their sons and daughters. At the end of the day, a child needs to grow up in a household where they feel love and support from both parents: two things that matter most during a child's developmental years.

I don't remember the first time I realized my father would no longer be a part of my life. My last interaction with my father was when I was 2 years old.

The next time he was brought up was when my mother told me she was no longer receiving child support from him and no one knew where he was. Imagine how hard this was to hear for a young boy. I grew up watching *The Cosby Show*, wishing Bill Cosby was my dad. Here was this fictional character on TV, giving the same love and support I referred to earlier to his five children. Imagine that: FIVE KIDS. He knew the behavior and tendencies of all his children.

> **"There were so many times when I wished I had that kind of man in my life—someone who would be there for me during my proudest moments and my times of struggle yet would love me just the same."**

He taught Vanessa a lesson when she came home intoxicated. He was there when Theo and Justine broke up, and he encouraged his son to sing a song entitled, "Justine, Justine." He interacted with Rudy and her young friends when they'd come over for slumber parties. He was even supportive of Denise when she wanted to go off to Africa to be a photographer's assistant. He was that kind of father that knew the highs and lows of all his children and treated them accordingly. There were so many times when I wished I had that kind of man in my life—someone who would be there for me during my proudest moments and my times of struggle yet would love me just the same.

Instead, I was dealing with a man that completely disappeared from my life.

It was during those tough moments that my mother made the decision to raise me on her own. She realized she didn't want a man around her son who didn't *truly* want to be active in his life. I'm not saying it didn't matter whether or not my father was there, I'm saying that *she* decided she would try her best in ensuring it didn't negatively affect my life. This decision involved several things:

1. She made the decision to support me financially on her own. I'm sure many single mothers out there know how tough it is to raise their children while hopping back and forth between

numerous jobs. My mother held down two to three jobs at a time while still doing her best to be there for me emotionally.

2. She would be the one to have the serious life talks with me. I'll get more into this in Chapter 12, but to sum it up, she was the one that had to break down topics like the "birds and the bees" and what it meant to really be a man. I know there are skeptics out there that believe a woman can't raise a boy on her own. They believe there are certain talks and situations that a woman won't know how to handle appropriately. However, I am here to tell you this myth isn't always true. I am proof that a woman can decide to parent on her own and still get it right.

3. She was ready to sacrifice her needs for my own. I know that mothers in two-parent households and mothers who share custody with the father

make these decisions, but I believe it holds a little more weight for women who are in it on their own. My mother was responsible for me, but I can only imagine what it would have been like for her if she had to take care of a handful of children, like many women do each day. NBA Hall of Famer Kareem Abdul-Jabbar once said, "I think that the good and the great are only separated by the willingness to sacrifice." My mother was one of the greats who knew what it took to get things done.

There are a multitude of other times when she put my needs before her own. I can remember one situation when I was around 7 years old. I knew she was hungry because, like me, she hadn't eaten anything since the previous day. It was time for breakfast, but there were only enough eggs and grits for one person. What did she do? She sacrificed for me because she wanted me to "go to school with a clear mind, an eager learning appetite, and a full stomach." At the time, I took that type of sacrifice for granted. I thought it was just what a mom was supposed to do for her child. As I got older, I realized there were an unfortunate amount of parents out there, both men and women, who never put their children's needs before their own. Those are the type of parents we should pray for and help create awareness for so they can help their children.

There were other moments when I was in elementary school and junior high school when I needed appropriate clothing because I began to grow pretty fast. It was all my mother could do to keep me clothed in garments that actually fit my body and feet. She would take on another job to make sure I had name-brand clothes like Duck Head, Levi, Guess Jeans, and Izod. I even remember when she bought me the Cross Color shorts that the young rap group Kris Kross used to wear. Each school year, she made sure that I had what I needed. It was almost as though she predicted greatness for me and wanted to ensure I had all the necessary things that would get me to my goal of success. I don't think I ever owned a pair of Jordans, but I had what I needed. My mother did her best with what she had. I couldn't ask for more than that.

When I reflect on what I was going through during that time, I understand that there are countless children and mothers that are going through those same types of situations. Think of all the women throughout history that decided they wouldn't let a fatherless home handicap their children and gave their offspring all they could when they could. That's love. That is the kind of selfless, unconditional love that many women around the world decide to give, even when they know it will drain them financially, emotionally, and mentally. They do it because they know they must; they do it because it is in their hearts.

My advice to individuals who are not going through these challenges is to reach out to others who are living in fatherless homes and see how you can help them prosper and how you can help lift them up. Whether you're living in a two-parent household or it's just you and your child, remember that we all need help in this journey through life. No one, I repeat, NO ONE should be too proud to receive a helping hand from someone else. This is how many successful projects and business deals are completed in the real world: Person A consults with Person B, Person B gives his opinion by mapping out the pros and cons of each choice, and then after a great deal of thought, Person A makes a decision. This also happens in your everyday life. Trying to make a large family dinner? You ask your son to help you in the kitchen. Trying to decide whether or not a man would be a positive influence in your life? You ask your sister for her opinion of his character. Not sure whether you should end a friendship with a classmate? You go to your mom for help. We should never be afraid to branch out on our own, but it also helps to have a *valuable* opinion from a quality person to help you along the way.

Finally, it's important to remember, if you are ever faced with the decision to parent on your own, whether or not by your own volition, you're really never alone. I want to end this chapter with a story about a Cherokee Indian boy and his father. The boy's father told his son that for him to become a man, he would have to participate in a test that all Indian boys have to go through to become a man. Each boy that transitioned into becoming a man that had passed this test could not share it with the other Indian boys. The boy was told that his father would take him far out into the woods away from the village. After they arrived in the woods, the father would blindfold the boy and have him sit on a stump. After he was blindfolded, the father would leave and go back to the village, and the boy would have to remain sitting on the stump the entire night by himself. The boy could not take the blindfold off or leave in order for him to make this transition.

After arriving deep in the woods, the boy was blindfolded, the father left, and then night finally came. While sitting there, the boy heard all types of noises. *Was that an animal that could attack him? Is that the sound of another Indian from another tribe that could kill him?* These questions ran through the young boy's mind, but he had to keep the blindfold on. Hours passed, and eventually, the boy felt the sunshine from the next day on his skin; he could see the brightness peek through the covering over his eyes. When he took the blindfold off of his eyes, he was surprised to see something: his father sitting across from him. Apparently, his father had sat out in the woods with his son the entire night, protecting him and making sure no harm came to him.

The moral of the story is that as we travel through this journey called life, just like the Indian boy, we are *never* alone; God is always by our side and protecting us. So, it is extremely important to remember that just because we can't see God, it doesn't mean he's not there.

God is always with us in the brightest of days and the darkest of nights. There's a saying that we should "walk by faith, and not by sight," and this is something that is true and that we all should remember. Whatever challenges we face in life, we are never alone. He wants to see us achieve all of our desires and all of our goals, and he is always with us as we continue this journey.

Chapter 4 – Making it Through Childhood

"She gets up while it is still dark; she provides food for her family and portions for her servant girls. She considers a field and buys it; out of her earnings she plants a vineyard. She sets about her work vigorously; her arms are strong for her tasks."

–Proverbs 31:15-17

Every day around the world, millions of children wake up in a household that doesn't have a father. Like the young boy asking his mother about his father in Chapter 1, many young people grow up questioning why their dad isn't there. Some believe it's something they did wrong to make him go away. Some get angry at the man that gave them life because he chose to disappear instead of playing an active role in their lives. Some worry about the stress it puts on their mother as she becomes solely responsible for raising her children.

I was that kid who thought all of those things.

I wondered why my father no longer paid child support to help take care of the basic necessities in my life. *Did I do something wrong to make him disappear? Will he ever come back?* I'd ask myself these questions over and over in my head when I was very young. I grew very angry at my absent father shortly before I became a teenager (something I'll go into more in Chapter 9 – "Getting Rid of Anger"). I couldn't understand why this man would totally disregard his first-born child, dismissing my existence as if I never really mattered. My anger had me acting out, something I'd later come to understand as emotional hurt and pain. And, as I finally grew older, my concern focused around the impact that single parenthood would have on my mother. Once I was able to move past my questioning and my anger at my father, I began to wonder how my mother was able to raise a child—a boy, no less—without having a male role model in the household. But she did it. She held her head high, and she did what she knew she had to do: be a mother to me.

One of the primary ways my mother was able to raise me to become an honorable, hardworking man was to surround me with love from family members who always had my back and supported me. Because I was my mother's only child, my closest family members were her parents, her three brothers, and her only sister. Because their roles were so important in assisting my mother in raising me, I would like to introduce them:

PawPaw

This is the name I call my grandfather. PawPaw was the main male influence in my life while growing up and is still very influential in my life today. I always call him the wealthiest man I know, not because he has millions of dollars, but because of his wisdom. He always turned a simple situation into a learning lesson and made certain that I maintained a good attitude, regardless of my circumstances. As a Baptist preacher, I'd always admired the way he could convey a message to his congregation; he would inspire them to stay encouraged, maintain faith, and live a better life. With all his influence, he was still always able to spend time with and talk to me on an individual basis to make sure I remained on the right track for success. PawPaw was the main male disciplinarian during my childhood years, as well. Momma's whippings would hurt, but I definitely didn't like being whipped by PawPaw! In addition to the discipline and mindset I gained from PawPaw's presence, he also showed me what a husband and father were supposed to look like. He and my grandmother have now been married for well over 50 years, so I have seen them go through ups and downs. But they committed to never quitting on their relationship. I also saw responsibility. He came home every day and made sure the bills were paid and the family had food to eat. My mother understood how important it was to ensure this man was always around me, uplifting me, and keeping me focused on my dreams.

Granny

My mother also made sure I had a great relationship with my grandmother, Granny. She is the backbone of the family—for as long as I can remember, she's always been the peacemaker and the glue that has kept my family together. During my childhood, Granny would always volunteer to watch me and take care of me whenever my mother had to work late or was not home for some reason. I learned a lot of life lessons from Granny. Sometimes growing up, it seemed that she could be a little overprotective, but I can appreciate why now. Not to say they lived in a bad neighborhood when I was younger, but Granny did not allow me to leave the yard when I was playing. Most of the kids in the neighborhood could roam the streets and come and go as they pleased, but not me. Granny made sure to keep me away from the wrong crowd of kids because she didn't want me getting into any trouble. So, that led me to things like having to play catch with myself by throwing the ball on top of the house and waiting for it to roll off to catch it. Like I said, it was tough then, but I appreciate Granny making sure I didn't get mixed up in the wrong crowd of kids. Granny also always listened to my stories and feelings about what may have been going on at home, and she helped me with my schoolwork. Most of all, Granny was the one who always reminded me to keep my focus on God and my faith. From the time I was old enough to remember, Granny always made sure I recognized that because of Him, we were blessed, and I should always focus on that. Anytime I ever had a problem or just needed to talk, I could always visit or call Granny. This fact is still true today. My childhood was very blessed to have someone like her present at all times.

Auntie Paulette

Auntie Paulette is my mother's only sister. Since I can remember, she was always the one who would love to have fun, fun, fun. She has always had a bubbly personality and would listen to anything I had to stay. In addition to Momma and Granny, Auntie Paulette was like a mother figure to me. In fact, my mother was working and attending a technical college after I came home from the hospital months after my birth, and Auntie Paulette would babysit me. The family always tells the story about how Auntie Paulette gave me my first hair cut. As a baby, I really didn't have any hair besides a very long strand that set right in the center of the top of my head. Well, after dressing me one day, Auntie Paulette thought I looked rather cute, but the one long strand of hair was messing up everything. So, she decided to cut it off! Momma and Granny were furious with her because in the black community, if you cut a baby's hair before their first birthday, it is supposed to impair them in some way. I'm glad this turned out not to be true in my case! But they always share this funny story. She has been married for more than 20 years to her husband, and I have also watched them successfully stay together over the years, despite their ups and downs. I could talk to her about the things I couldn't talk to Momma and Granny about. This is also exemplified later in the book.

Uncle Kevin

Uncle Kevin is my mother's youngest brother. Out of all of my uncles, he and I were the closest. Uncle Kevin would take me around the neighborhood and to the mall with him. He would take me everywhere. Then, one day, I realized that it was probably because I made him look better to all the ladies, and that was fine because I also liked the attention. When I was very young, prior to him being married, I thought he was the ultimate ladies man. He could dress well, always had a clean car, and seemed super confident. I believe this shaped my confidence when it came to dating and my swagger. Uncle Kevin has also been married for more than 20 years to the same woman and this taught me that although you can be a ladies man, you could still settle down eventually and become a responsible husband and father. Uncle Kevin also was an advocate who encouraged me to play sports, like he did growing up.

Uncle Orsola

Uncle Orsola is my mother's middle brother. This uncle taught me to appreciate nature and not just depend on the finer things in life to get me by. He taught me how to fish, bought me my first BB gun, and taught me how live off the land.

I remember the first time I went fishing with Uncle Orsola and my younger cousin Mon, his son. After driving for miles on a dirt road deep in the country, we parked along the side of the road and started walking through the woods to get to the lake. It seemed like it took us days to get to the actual lake. The temperature outside that day was super hot and the mosquitoes were tearing me up. We stayed all day long until nightfall. We made a campfire while we continued to enjoy Swiss Roll Debbie cakes, Lays plain potato chips, Barrel bottle juices, bananas, and sardines with hot sauce! Later that night, this diet caused my stomach to feel bad, and it was time to go to the bathroom. But because we were out in no man's land, I started to grow concerned!

As my stomach continued to turn, I couldn't take it anymore and walked a few yards away to go. As I finally found relief and was ready to finish this process, I asked my uncle if he had brought some toilet tissue. His response was, "Boy, we're living on the land today! Use some leaves!"

At this point, I just started crying. There was no way I was going to clean myself with some leaves.

There's more to the story, but I'll spare you the gruesome details. Needless to say, every fishing trip thereafter, I brought my own toilet paper.

Uncle June

Finally, my mother's oldest brother is James Jr., whom I called Uncle June. I assume I called him this because I couldn't correctly say "Junior" when I was a toddler. Out of all the personalities in my family, he was the most subdued and easy going. If fact, he lived very modestly and spent hardly any money on anything it seemed. I would love to go over to his home in my pre-teen years because he didn't monitor what I watched on TV and left out his adult movie collection and adult magazines. At that age, I shouldn't have been looking at those things. He had stated a few times that he wanted to make sure I could get familiar with the female anatomy early so I wouldn't turn out becoming a homosexual because I was being raised by a woman. I don't think this was the right way of doing it, but he accomplished his goal for the contribution he made.

The purpose of sharing all of this information with you about my closest family members was to maybe help you think of individuals close to you that are similar that could assist in helping raise your child or influence you if you are the child reading this book. It is a full-time job raising a child, and it is equally tough, believe it or not, on the child when the father is not around.

Although I had mixed emotions about my father not being around, it was something I was used to. One reason was because it had always been like that—my father wasn't active in my life, so it was Momma and me against the world, although I had the love and support of my family members.   The   second reason was that almost everyone I knew was growing up in a single-parent household. Unfortunately, they were probably going through the same host of emotions I dealt with but each in their own way. My boys from the neighborhood, the girls in my English class, the kids I'd see at the park—a good number of us didn't have our fathers around.

It saddens me to know that countless children before my life, during my childhood, and those living today are growing up without their father playing an active role in their lives. Statistically, boys that grow up without fathers are more likely to wind up in gangs, become involved in illegal activity, and wind up in prison, whereas a young girl may grow up to have emotional conflicts and relationship issues with men due to her father never teaching her what she should and should not accept from a man. However, to many of us in the neighborhood, we didn't see ourselves as potential statistics. We just saw ourselves as normal. Why? Everyone else was going through the same thing; everyone else didn't have a father.

Imagine how something can seem entirely normal, even when it shouldn't be. This is comparable to people thinking it is OK to pay $300 for a pair of LeBron James shoes when they have a hard time putting food on the table. If the general consensus is that something is the standard, or correct, it is easily accepted by everyone else. However, this goes back to the idea that just because it's accepted by everyone else, doesn't make it OK. And just because a lot of us didn't have our fathers around, didn't mean we were living in an ideal situation.

Growing up in the projects, I learned how dedicated the mothers around me were, especially my mom. Her character and devotion to me shone brightly as she made selfless acts to ensure I was taken care of. I can remember times when our car was broken down and she'd walk to her different jobs, which were miles away from each other. There were countless times she'd walk me to school, but not before I had a hot breakfast in my stomach. She wanted to ensure I arrived at school safely and ready to learn.

I also remember how she only wanted to bring me good news, never wanting me exposed to the harsh realities of our life in the projects and some of the financial struggles she was going through. I remember, one time in particular, when we came home and the lights and heat were off.

"What happened to the lights, Momma?" I remember asking her.

"You know what? I forgot to tell you! We are going camping tonight, right here in the apartment," she responded. "Go get us some flashlights, sleeping bags, and blankets, and I'll make our tent in the living room."

"Ok, Momma! This is going to be great!" I responded before running off to get the supplies.

I had so much fun sleeping the night away that evening, not knowing until later in life the real reason why the heat and lights were off: she didn't have enough money to pay these bills until the weekend. However, she realized that there was no point in sharing this bad news with me because I'd probably end up confused or concerned. In situations like these, she took her struggles up to God. My mother gave of herself in countless ways, all in an attempt to make life better for me.

There are countless mothers around the world right now that are exactly like my mother. They understand how crucial it is to create a loving environment in their home so their children will flourish academically, physically, emotionally, and spiritually. It's no easy task to raise children on your own, as I'm sure many of you reading may know. It's not only physically draining, but it can be emotionally and mentally draining, as well. I understand how dark each day may appear, realizing you are responsible for raising that young man or young lady to be someone you will be proud of one day. I know my success was a noteworthy dream for my mother, as it is for all of you.

As I reflect on how my mother pushed me to advance in life, I see how she ensured I had the appropriate things available so I would continue to grow. Here are some things my mother made sure I had in my life—these are options you may be able to apply to your life:

1. **She kept positive male role models around me**. This was probably the most important step in my development from a boy to a man—to have male family members who cared about my well-being to surround me with love and

encouragement. When I grew up, my uncles and grandfather were always supportive of me. They gave me the attention I needed from a man. With them, I could talk sports, learn the appropriate ways to treat a girl, and discuss certain issues I wasn't comfortable talking about with my mom. Yes, my mother was my primary caregiver, but she knew (as I slowly began to realize during my formative years) that there was advice she wouldn't be able to give me but knew those men could. She understood there were conversations that wouldn't hit me the same way as when my uncle would have them with me. These men were all imperative in my transformation into a young man.

For all the mothers out there, both young and old, it's important to recognize the value of positive male role models in the life of a child. There are many women who believe that they can "do it on my own without a man." And they'd be right; they *can* do it on their own without the help of the child's father. However, rearing a child becomes far easier when strong men are present in children's lives. You can drive a car with one hand. You can make iced tea without sugar. You can even make a peanut butter sandwich without jelly. Nevertheless, when you have that extra ingredient—when you have that extra *something*–it makes things so much easier. I would encourage you to find that positive male role model for your child, your brother or sister, your fatherless friend, or even yourself and make sure you keep them close to you. They are indispensable figures that can help pave the road to a successful and rewarding life.

2. **She prevented the things we lacked from hindering my growth.** My mother made sure that

our financial hardships didn't affect me too much. She never asked me for money because she believed she was the one who was supposed to take care of me, not the other way around. As I mentioned earlier, she made our lights getting turned off a game. She didn't want me worrying about things I could not control. She didn't want me feeling uncomfortable because we were sitting in the dark at night instead of having light surrounding us while at the apartment. It was almost as though she wanted me to not notice something that was sometimes a part of our living situation, and for that, I am thankful.

I'm sure there are many parents whose living situations are very complicated, more than the lights being turned off or the family car being out of commission. Yet, I'd offer this advice: Don't let the negative situations you're dealing with as an adult affect the livelihood of your child. I am painfully aware that this cannot always be done. Sometimes your children will experience the same pain you experience. But if there are ways to keep them away from the trials that many parents go through, keep them at bay. In the end, you will have protected them from the downfalls adults go through, and they won't look at adverse life experiences with a jaded point of view, thus allowing it to affect their life and their future.

At the end of the day, I realize my childhood was much like those of my peers growing up, and it's similar to the lives of children across the globe. Whether someone is growing up in an abusive household or lacks emotional support from their parents, making it through childhood can be a difficult task. Still, I believe with the appropriate tools, whether it is a close-knit family, steadfast male role model, or being protected from the challenges adults face, a child can come out on top and live a rewarding and fulfilling life as they mature. There's a saying that states, "Anything worth having is worth fighting for." When it comes to ensuring a child has positive experiences early on in life, this quote rings true—a great childhood is worth fighting for.

Chapter 5 – What Sports Teach a Boy

"My motto was always to keep swinging. Whether I was in a slump or feeling badly or having trouble off the field, the only thing to do was keep swinging."

–Hank Aaron, Entrepreneur and Baseball Legend

One fall evening in McDonough, Georgia at the local baseball park, the last game of the season was taking place for the 7- to 8-year-old little league before the playoffs. I was playing for one of the teams that night, the McDonough Dodgers. We had a pretty successful season, but this night was the deciding game on whether or not we would make the playoffs, and the tension was high. This game was the ultimate goal for players all around the area. Any athlete can tell you the main point of competing in a league is to win a championship, and this is what we were focused on. We wanted to win. During this particular game, both teams fought hard, and at the bottom of the final inning, we were down with a score of 6-3.

My teammates and I were getting nervous. Our coach paced back and forth in the dugout, wanting our team to be victorious so he could storm the field with us in celebration. We were all on edge. My teammates went up to the plate and got on base, and before we knew it, the bases were loaded. However, through the course of loading the bases, we also accrued two outs. So we were one out away from the end of our season. Without even paying much attention, the unthinkable happened next.

"Now batting: number five, Reco McDaniel," the announcer said over the intercom.

I'll tell you right now, I was nervous. When I say nervous, I mean my legs felt like they were made of rubber, my palms were beginning to sweat, and my heart felt like an African tribal drum inside my chest. As the smallest guy on the team, I am pretty sure many people didn't believe I could contribute something significant in this crucial situation. I felt like I couldn't catch my breath as I approached the plate; I was so anxious. As I stepped into the batter's box, I looked into the dugout and noticed my coach also appeared to be very uneasy. His eyes were rapidly shifting back and forth between me and the pitcher, and I noticed he had droplets of sweat on his brow. Imagine seeing your coach more nervous than you! It's a feeling that can be truly overwhelming, especially in a situation like this. As I sized up my opponent, the pitcher, I said a little prayer to myself and dug my cleats into the red clay at home plate.

The pitcher began his wind up and threw to the catcher. The ball flew past me.

"Strike One!" the umpire shouted.

Man, I better get it together, I thought to myself. *Just breathe, Reco. Just breathe.*

The pitcher threw again, this time a curveball.

"Strike Two!" I heard the umpire say.

OK, man, it's do or die right now. The bases are loaded, and you can be a hero. Just focus. Be patient. Help me Jesus! I said internally.

The pitcher threw ball one, ball two, and before I knew it, there was a full count. With his next pitch, the game could essentially be over.

I had to focus.

As he wound up for his next pitch, the voice of my mother and grandmother came into my mind. "You can do all things through Christ who strengthens you," I heard them say. "You were built for moments like these; your full armor is on and you are ready." And with that, I kept my focus on the fastball headed my way and swung away.

The next thing I knew, I felt and heard my bat connect with the baseball. As I started my frantic run around the bases, I noticed the ball was still flying and sailed over the outfield wall. I had hit a grand slam, winning the game for my team with a score of 7-6. As I rounded third base on my trot to home plate, all of my teammates waited for me with looks of pure elation on their faces. Everything seemed to go into slow motion; I can remember seeing everyone jumping up and down, with a few of them throwing their gloves and hats in the air. Even my coach was there with the biggest smile on his face that I had ever seen.

I had come through in the clutch for my team, despite my small stature. I believed enough in myself, and my dream came true. After winning that game, we entered the playoffs, beating each team that followed and eventually winning the championship!

I remember how proud my mother was of me after that game, knowing that we hardly had money to pay for registration at the beginning of the baseball season to her child becoming the hero for his team at the end of the season. I could tell her heart was filled with joy. I'm grateful that she took whatever available resources we had to ensure that I was able to participate in sports.

Reflecting on that moment later in life, I realize how bad I wanted to succeed—for myself and, even more importantly, for my mother. I knew that many people didn't believe I had a chance of making a noteworthy impact, but I was determined to prove to them that I could. This was one of the biggest defining moments in my life.

Like many young boys across the United States, sports played a major role in my life growing up. Some boys wanted to play video games, whereas others wanted to hang with their friends after school to see what they could get into. But for me, sports were my outlet. Sports allowed me to express myself while, at the same time, teaching me valuable lessons.

Although I didn't know my father, I believed— along with many of my family members—that my athletic abilities came from him. Although I enjoyed playing a variety of sports, such as basketball and football, I thoroughly enjoyed and excelled in baseball. It allowed me to show off my fielding abilities, as well as my throwing arm, my speed around the bases, and my power with the bat at the plate. I was focused on this sport from elementary school all the way into high school, always desiring to gun someone out from center field as they attempted to round third base for home plate. Baseball was a channel that allowed me to learn important life lessons. Over time, I realized that participating in sports taught me a variety of things.

By playing sports, I began to understand the importance of teamwork and started to identify with the concept of leadership. Understanding these two elements and learning conceptually how to implement them in any organization is the difference between someone getting a job or having a career. A job may be able to pay your bills, but you can pay your bills and enjoy your lifestyle with a career. Teamwork taught me how to work with others that may have different personalities, but we could still achieve the same goal. I also found out that I enjoyed leading, inspiring, and motivating others to reach their full potential. This is very important because if a child figures this out early in life, they will operate at a very high level in life by setting an example for others. You have two options in how to live your life: 1) as a warning, with people looking at your life and being warned as how not to live; or 2) as an example, with people looking at your life and seeing an example of how they would like to live. So, choose to lead by example. Leaders influence our schools, our communities, our country, and even our world.

Second, sports showed me there will always be winners and non-winners in sports, as well as life. In life, some would say that there are people who start off their lives as pure "winners"— they'll grow up in a stable household, where they are financially stable, will never go to bed hungry, and will take family vacations during their summer breaks. They'll be able to shop at Macy's and Polo and go to Foot Locker and buy designer shoes, have their parents attend their debate matches, and will be socially and academically successful. In short, they will be the champions. Then there are the "non-winners," the ones who have to fight for everything they have. These individuals may be ashamed of their clothing because they're forced to wear them, although they've outgrown the items. Financially, their family struggles to pay the rent, the utilities, and other monthly responsibilities. Society will subconsciously tell them they're not as good as the winners, a fact that couldn't be further from the truth. This group of people will struggle with feelings of inadequacy when they're around their peers or associates who have all the things they don't: Money. Status. Prestige.

> **"Just because you start out behind the curve doesn't mean it will always be like that."**

This comparison is similar to many professional sports teams from around the United States. It's the difference between the Los Angeles Lakers and the Indiana Pacers, the New York Yankees and the Houston Astros, and the New England Patriots and the Cincinnati Bengals. Some will seem to always have the winning hand, whereas the others fight to survive.

Next, sports showed me that although someone can start off as a seemingly non-winner, it doesn't mean they have to remain that way. Always remember this: Where you are, does not define who you are. Who you are is defined by what's in your mind and the vision you have for yourself. Look at me as an example. I started the game of life as an underprivileged boy who was fighting to survive with his mother. We couldn't afford the new Jordans when the shoe became popular in the late 1980s and during the 1990s. We weren't taking family vacations to Disney World or making a road trip to witness

Niagara Falls up close. And as much as I wanted to, we weren't sitting in box seats at Falcons games. And I sure wasn't on the golf course playing 18 holes while having fun with my friends and associates.

However, these are all options for me and my family now.

I may have started the game of life as an underdog, but with a good foundation provided by my mother, work on my part, and, most importantly, God on my side, I have been tremendously blessed and my life has transformed! Again, I'd like to drive this point across over and over: Just because you start out behind the curve doesn't mean it will always be like that. Similar to the 1990 Atlanta Braves, you can start off in last place one year, just to turn it all around and be in first place the following year. Even the New England Patriots quarterback, Tom Brady, went from worst to first: in the 2000 NFL draft, he was picked in the sixth round and was the 199th overall pick. This man went on to lead one of the most competitive teams in the NFL, is a seven-time Pro Bowler, won five AFC titles, and won three Super Bowl rings by the time he was 30 years old. He is arguably one of the top three quarterbacks in the NFL today, and it all started with a 6'4", 215-lb kid from the University of Michigan, who had a dream to work as hard as he could and prove his critics and competitors wrong.

Life is like March Madness in college basketball, anything can happen. Expect the unexpected.

Additionally, sports taught me to be competitive. There were so many times during my high school sports career where my team became intimidated when we saw the opposing team. Their guys may have been taller, faster, or more talented. Their blue-chip pitcher may have thrown an 86-mph fastball, something none of our pitchers were capable of doing. Although I was pretty quick around the bases, there were guys from schools in my district that could outrun me. Some may have had better throwing arms, and some teams were superior to ours. Most times, they knew it. However, our competitive nature forced us to compete and still win. We were determined not to give up just because the other team held advantages over us. We took the competition as a challenge to

> **"...you will be the underdog. They may have certain physical or mental advantages that may intimidate you. However, you shouldn't let that stop you from giving your all and facing the competitor head on. In life, you either win or you *learn*, but you never lose—it's all about your perspective."**

make us better as a team, no matter what the end result was.

This same lesson should be applied to real-life situations. There will be times when you'll have to compete against people who *seem* to have an advantage over you. In short, you will be the underdog. They may have certain physical or mental advantages that may intimidate you. However, you shouldn't let that stop you from giving your all and facing the competitor head on. In life, you either win or you *learn*, but you never lose—it's all about your perspective. When someone focuses on the loss, they tend to get depressed and feel inferior. That's why it is important to enter the competition expecting to win or learn. If you win, great! It's on to the next challenge.

If you don't win, that's okay. You just learned how to prepare better for the next opportunity. This is applied to sports and all areas of your life.

In the 2012 NBA Finals, the Oklahoma City Thunder went up against the Miami Heat. Miami had arguably better players (two being household names before the series), were nationally recognized favorites to win the championship at the beginning of the season, and had a fan base that grew in size with the acquisition of two-time NBA MVP and eight-time all-star, LeBron James. Oklahoma had great players, as well, but most of their squad was young and not as seasoned as those 12 guys who played in South Beach, Florida.

Sure, the Thunder eventually lost the five-game series to the Heat, but look at it this way—was anyone even thinking about Oklahoma 3 years before that series? Did anyone truly believe the team would be playing in a finals game when they were relocated from Seattle to Oklahoma City? No, no one (except for their management team) could have foreseen how far the team would come in a few short years. When it was all said and done, this team was the second best team in the NBA, even if they did lose the series in the end. But again, it's all about perspective. The Thunder could have looked at themselves as losers or as a squad that *learned* something about their character, sportsmanship, dedication to the game, and how to better prepare for their next chance. That alone is commendable. Those lessons take heart.

Finally, sports taught me one final lesson that is required if you want to succeed at a high level in almost anything you do: confidence. As I stated earlier, I wanted to win, and I was competitive. But after I started winning, I had an attitude of not only did I want to win, but I also knew I could win. If you enter any situation with positive expectations and an attitude that you will come out on top, you give yourself an edge that your competition may not have. Confidence for someone who wants to succeed is just as important as a parachute for someone who is jumping out a plane. If you don't have it, the result may not be too pretty! So, have an attitude that you can win, but make sure you learn what's necessary to win. This is where I learned the difference between confidence and competence. Many people don't know the difference between the two, but activities like sports can clarify this for young boys (and young girls) that are showing up in need of discipline. Some people think just because they're confident, they will succeed, but this isn't true. You must also know how to succeed; your attitude about succeeding will just assist you getting there faster. So confidence is a function of attitude, whereas competence is a function of ability. My competence, or my ability to perform in my daily activities, increased, as well, because of my new level of understanding I attained from sports. From earning straight A's in the classroom to singing in the church choir, my competence grew with each year I participated in baseball, football, and basketball. These two areas helped to create the structure I needed for my journey from a boy to a man.

Overall, the lessons a young man can learn from sports can help influence the way he views the world around him. Sports supply discipline that is otherwise missing for some boys, especially those like me who grow up without their fathers. A sport helps to shape one's character and teach a young person the definition of hard work, sharpens their work ethic, and shows them the value of teamwork. It also proves that we may not all start off in the game of life as winners, but that doesn't mean we can't become one. Each person can become the hope in the unseen.

Everyone loves an underdog story. Yours can be the one that inspires an entire nation.

Chapter 6 – You Will Work...

"Opportunity is missed by most people because it is dressed in overalls and looks like work."
–Thomas Edison, American Businessman and Inventor

My mother was a real stickler when it came to me having a job. When I turned 14 years old, she told me it was time to get a job. For many kids around this age, they dread the moment when their parents tell them it's time to make their own money. It's easy to see how kids enjoy having their parents hold down all the financial responsibilities for the family! However, I was genuinely excited to start this next chapter in my life. I was ready to begin my journey into the world of financial responsibility and independence, and my mother was the catalyst that started it all.

Because my mother never sat around with idle hands, it was easy for me to make the transition from Reco McDaniel, high school student, to Reco McDaniel, high school student and working young man! Before I started putting in time at a job, my mother made sure to teach me the importance of financial independence. She understood that it was one thing to tell a child to go out and get a job, but it was another thing to teach them how to be responsible with their money and either save it or invest it in themselves. Before I started working, she

> **"...my mother showed me the importance of independence at a time where many young people still believed they should have every expense covered by their parents."**

helped me open a bank account and taught me how to balance my checkbook, ensuring I was keeping track of the money coming in and leaving my account.

She was of the belief that it was OK for her to take care of the household responsibilities, such as paying the mortgage, taking care of the utilities, and covering the maintenance of our house. However, she told me it was my responsibility to take care of *my* needs: this included clothing and shoes I wanted, fees for yearbooks and other graduation activities, and any field trip or school activities I wanted to attend. Looking back on it, my mother showed me the importance of independence at a time where many young people still believed they should have every expense covered by their parents.

My first real job was at the ever-so-popular McDonalds. I was 14 years old and, like many kids my age, worked on fries and flipped burgers on the weekends. Although it wasn't the most luxurious job in the world, it taught me an important lesson about leadership. I know you may be thinking, "What can McDonalds teach someone about leadership when they're taking orders at the drive-thru?" My response is this: It taught me to be accountable for myself, it showed me how to interact with co-workers, and like sports, it taught me the importance of teamwork. After a period of time, my managers saw what a hard worker I was and promoted me to head cashier on the weekends. Again, at the time, this was a big deal for me. I felt a sense of accomplishment as I performed my job duties day in and day out.

The summer before getting hired at McDonalds, I was also in a technical skills program that my mother believed would help build my work ethic called JTPA. The program would go from 8 a.m. to 11 a.m. and would teach us practical work proficiency and then transport us to different job sites around the city, where we worked from 12 p.m. to 5 p.m. My job sites fluctuated between an elementary and middle school in the area. My job duties for the day depended on whether I wanted to work inside in the air-conditioned classrooms or work outside in 100-degree humid summer heat.

"Reco, you want to be inside or outside today?" the job coordinator asked me.

"I think I'll work inside today. It's too hot to be outside. What will I have to do?" I asked, waiting to hear my duty.

"Well, you'll be inside scraping gum from the bottom of the students' desks. We need it all completed before we leave today," she replied.

And so, I would move from classroom to classroom getting the gum from the bottom of the desks with a scraper, which seemed to be the cheapest scraping tool they could purchase. This went on from noon until the van pulled off at 5 p.m. I know some of you may think, "you did that for 5 hours?!?" But I'll say this: sometimes this was better than shoveling wood chips and picking up trash in humid, sticky 100-degree weather in the recess areas of the school.

There were many days that I would come home and complain and want to quit. My mother would always explain that life wasn't going to be easy, so I was going have to get prepared for it. I can remember, like it was yesterday, when she would tell me, "No one is going to take care of you. You will have to take care of yourself. So, you will work!"

As stated earlier, my mother was truly proud that I continued to work and prided myself in making my own money. There was no prouder moment for me than getting my paycheck every 2 weeks and knowing I had earned that. Instead of going out and buying the newest, most popular pair of shoes or video games, I chose to save my money in my bank account. Little did I know this conscious decision would change the way my mother saw me.

When I was 15 years old, I came into the living room to see my mother sitting on the couch with her head in her hands and bills spilled all around the table in front of her. I knew what this kind of moment meant—as I had grown older, I was able to identify it as a moment where my mother was trying to figure how she'd pay the impending bills. Like the camping story I discussed in the chapter "Making it Through Childhood," my mother did not want to concern me with bills. She protected me from these types of things and took her worries to God.

"What's wrong, Momma?" I asked her.

"I've got these bills to pay, and I know I won't have enough to cover these last two," she said pointing at the heat and water bills.

"Momma, I can help you pay these. I have some money."

She shook her head profusely. "Reco, I don't want your money. That's yours. This is *my* responsibility. With God, I will figure this out. It will work out."

"But, Momma, I can help you. I've been saving."

"Reco, I'm not going to take your last $75. Thank you for offering, though. It'll be OK."

After seeing that she didn't believe that I had enough money to help her, I went to my room, grabbed my checkbook, and headed back to the living room.

"Look, Momma, I have enough."

Her eyes fell to the item I had in my hand, and she slowly took it from me. Her gaze ran over the numbers I had in the book, and after a while, she looked up at me in disbelief. She couldn't believe what she had read.

"Reco, this checkbook says you have over $1,000 in your account. You have more money in your checking account than I do!" I remember her saying in amazement. "I may be able to make this work."

At that moment, I felt good. My entire life, my mother had taken care of me. From the obstacles that I faced at birth to ensuring I had every necessity I needed, my mother provided. It was a no-brainer that it was *my* turn to help her. Because I had come to the age that I could make a difference in her life, I jumped at the opportunity.

My mother's insistence on having a job proved to be a great thing for both me and her. Little did we both know when I started earning my own money that I'd be able to contribute to our household responsibilities. This same theory can be applied to parents raising teenage children today. Although a child may challenge your decision to have them work, it will be a great thing for them because it will teach discipline, responsibility, and independence. When a child gets a paycheck, it helps them understand how hard it can be to make the money and how quickly the money can disappear if it's not spent and saved wisely.

The importance of teaching these lessons to young men and women of working age is crucial in their development into hardworking members of the society.

I am so grateful that my mother taught me that the only person that was responsible for taking care of me was me. Sure, we all need help sometimes, but that does not excuse us from our responsibility to take care of ourselves. I saw this firsthand over the years, especially in my earlier years when we struggled most financially. Whenever my mother was without a job, while she constantly pursued a job by going to interview after interview, we were provided government assistance. From a housing allowance to food stamps, it really helped when we didn't have it. But my mother didn't get comfortable and just expect this assistance to take care of us because she assumed responsibility for our small family. We never had that assistance more than a few months because she was on to her next job.

I can say with complete certainty that the work ethic I possess, the independence and perseverance that I display, and the attitude on responsibility that I have, is a direct result of what I learned from my mother. I would have never gained the success I've been blessed with without having been taught these principals.

Therefore, in my opinion, all children should have responsibilities and "jobs," no matter the age. They should start early. As I explained to my 11-year-old son not long ago after a discussion, where I had to discipline him for something he had done, I explained to him, "You have a job!" His mother and I work to make sure we can provide shelter, clothing, food, entertainment, and a stable future for him and his sister. He then agreed that we do a good job because he never has to worry about the lights or heat being off, unclean or too small clothes to wear, being hungry, or a lack of fun and adventure. So, if we are doing our jobs to the best of our ability, so will he. His job, at this time, is to go to school, behave, make good grades, respect his peers, and give his best to any and all activities he is involved with. That is the expectation. That is his job. And I made it clear that he will work. My two-year-old daughter has a job. She is to make sure she doesn't potty in her clothes, be nice to her brother, and continue to be my princess. She knows her job.

The question you should ask yourself is, "What is my job? Am I doing it to the best of my ability?"

If you're a parent, ask yourself, "What is my child's job? Am I teaching them responsibility now?" This could change the dynamics of your home and your life.

The Fatherless Father

Chapter 7 – Discipline from Fear

"Discipline yourself, and others won't need to."
—John Wooden, Hall of Fame Basketball Coach

Fear is a powerful thing. It prevents someone from overcoming their anxiety of heights, whereas it keeps a child awake at night because of what is under their bed. Fear has the power to start wars, cause a stampede when danger is near, and change the history of a civilization. It causes an individual to vote for a certain candidate for fear of the laws the other politician will institute; it will make someone lose a tremendous amount of weight to fight off diabetes, high blood pressure, or maybe even death.

However you want to look at it, fear has the power to change behaviors. In a negative sense, fear can make you a prisoner in your own mind by limiting your potential to deal with certain aspects of your life.

Fear can also be good at times. This kind of fear sets boundaries and allows you to recognize and respect authority. Boundaries are set to protect us from danger and things that may not be good for us.

If it were not for the fear of law enforcement, our society might be filled with more crime and more hooligans. People respect the boundaries of the laws that are set because of the fear of going to jail, being fined, or the embarrassment of having to perform public community service. The laws are clear boundaries that citizens of the United States must abide by to avoid consequences. Likewise, most Christians possess a fear of God and abide by the boundaries set by the Holy Bible to avoid a lifetime spent burning in eternal fire. This type of fear causes a certain amount of discipline. This discipline prevents people from crossing boundaries to avoid experiencing unwanted consequences. This is the fear that should be instilled in our youth by their parents—discipline-provoking fear.

During my developmental years, my mother always used this fear to keep me in line. From the very beginning of my life, she always taught me that there are positive and negative consequences to my actions, and I definitely didn't want to experience those negative consequences! Ultimately, she wanted to instill discipline in my life and make me aware that if I did something wrong, there would be an undesirable experience waiting for me. That fear was something that kept me in line and prevented me from getting into some of the trouble, as I grew older, that I saw some of my friends getting into.

When I was a young boy, she'd be that constant reminder of why getting into trouble was not an option because she'd be there to discipline me both verbally and with a whipping. I remember my first real whipping like it was yesterday. Ever since I can remember, Momma was always making sure I was accountable for my actions, whether she said stop or lightly popped my hand as a toddler, but up until the age of 4, I had never really endured anything worse than a few pops to the legs. On a Fall Saturday evening in 1985, all of that changed.

Granny, PawPaw, Momma, a few of my cousins, and I were all headed to Shoney's Restaurant, and I couldn't be more excited. It wasn't a common occurrence for us to go to "sit down" restaurants, so when we did, it was a big deal. We would all get dressed up to look our best for the occasion. On this particular day, I was wearing my leather pants, white socks, black loafers, red sweater, and sunglasses. As we began to get out of the car after arriving at the restaurant, I noticed I dropped something, my little white glove with rhinestones on it.

If you grew up in the 1980s, you'd understand why I was a fan of the greatest pop artist of all time, Michael Jackson, and the significance of a white glove like that. For some reason, I was really feeling like M. J. that day. I wanted to perform!

"Reco, stop singing while you're in the restaurant. That's rude, and people are trying to eat," Momma requested in a low, demanding tone.

"Yes ma'am," I responded, although I was still singing the song to myself. As I continued to rock from side to side with "Beat It" jamming in my head, I noticed a couple of girls my age sitting behind me that seemed to find my singing and outfit rather intriguing. They were smiling at me and looking as if they were waiting for me to do something to entertain them.

So when Momma and Granny went to the salad bar, I decided to do what Michael Jackson would do—perform.

As I stood up in my chair, the words started coming out of my mouth again, "It doesn't matter whose wrong or right, just beat it! Beat it! Just beat it! Beat it!"

As the girls started clapping, I felt the need to continue to perform, so I jumped on the table and started moon-walking a short distance and ending it with a loud, "WoooHoooo!"

After my 2 minutes of fame, I noticed that everyone on that side of the restaurant was looking at me in total disbelief, and I soon realized my decision wasn't such a great one. The next thing I remember is being yanked from the table like a tornado taking off the roof of a house in a violent thunderstorm.

Momma wasn't too pleased with my performance or my rendition of "Beat It." In fact, the only thing about to get beat was me!

That day, I got my first real whipping in the bathroom of Shoney's Restaurant. From then on, I knew that my mother was serious when she told me not to do something. Although my mother whipped me, she always told me why I was getting punished and explained that she was doing it because she loved me. It took many years to understand how she could love me and yet whip me, but I later understood that she was setting boundaries early in my life so I would recognize and respect authority later in life.

As I got older, I tried to talk *over* her when she was trying to teach me a lesson. You know how it goes—your mother is telling you how it was wrong for you to not turn in your homework, but you've got every excuse under the sun as to why it wasn't done. You hear her speaking to you but you start raising your voice, trying desperately to win the argument. However, my mother would not be outdone. She would be heard whether I liked it or not. Although I was getting older, that still didn't mean I would have the power to dominate her in conversation when she was sharing something important for me to hear and understand. One of the sayings I remember hearing most when we had a disagreement in my teenage years was, "As long as you live under my roof, you will abide by my rules!" She may have been small in her 5'3" stature, but she made up for that with her large set of rules that I was required to abide by.

The discipline I learned from fear helped me to make good decisions when I was away from my

> **"...the fear I had of my mother helped me to make conscious decisions in my life."**

mother. As I transitioned from a young boy into a young man, Momma understood that she could only be around me so much. Yes, she was there every night when I came home from school or my job, but as I became a teenager and had the ability to go to more places on my own, she was not there with me. It was during those times that the lessons I learned from her came into play. It was then that I had to remember the discipline she imparted on me and apply them to real-world situations. When I saw some of my classmates disrespecting the teacher, I stayed away from them, knowing it was not the proper thing to do. When I would see them using drugs and drinking, I put some distance between me and them, knowing that it was the right thing to do, but also realizing that my mother would have told me to do this. (What's interesting is that these same people who participated in these negative behaviors during childhood haven't progressed in life—they're the same guys who are still hanging out in the old neighborhood, wishing they had more positive options for their lives.)

As I travel the country and visit various cities around the world, I notice the extreme need for discipline in the lives of some of the youth today. I'm not sure where things went wrong, but I've witnessed kids acting out in malls, in the grocery store, and even in school or church—two places where I was taught to be on my best behavior. I'm sure some of you reading this book have seen it, too, and have often times asked, "Where is this child's mother?" It's often a question that is asked internally but never stated out loud for fear that the child may act out on you. When I was growing up, kids knew that if your mother wasn't there to discipline you, someone else would *and* would tell your mother what you did! There was fear of the consequences that would bring. This unspoken rule, however, is no longer applicable in many places around the United States.

So you may ask, "Reco, how can we help curve this problem? What can be done to help put the youth of this country back on the right track?" I will admit the answer to this problem isn't a simple one; however, if the steps below are applied consistently and thoroughly, I believe the old-school discipline from yesteryear will help the youth of today.

First, parents need to set up a **list of expectations** for their children. These expectations need to be set up very early in the child's life so they'll abide by the rules as they progress through their life. Make up your bed every morning. Don't knowingly harm someone. Don't take something that is not yours. Say please and thank you, always. Don't cheat on your assignments and tests at school. Watch your language and pay attention to the words coming out of your mouth. Do not run wild in the store when we go inside. All of these expectations are simple in nature but go a long way in instilling discipline in a child's life.

During this time, parents will show the child that there is a right and wrong answer to any situation, and they always have a choice in the decision. My mother taught me that I would always be required to respect my elders, whether I liked them or not. I was fearful of what would happen to me if I chose to act up with an adult in my presence. She also schooled me on the importance being home before the streetlights came on. As an active young man, I always enjoyed playing outside with my friends; however, I knew that when those street lights started to come on, I needed to be in my house. I can recall practically flying home, running as fast as I could to ensure I would beat the lights. I knew what was waiting for me if I didn't get there when I was supposed to. These expectations were critical in molding me into the man I am today.

Next, it is important for parents to **instill responsibility** in their children. It doesn't matter how young the child is; it's important they understand they are accountable for certain things. However, the key is to instill this at a very early age so that the child will not deter from it as they get older. As I stated in the last chapter, my 11-year-old son has a job, or responsibilities that we expect him to take care of. For example, in addition to the things I mentioned earlier, it is my son's responsibility to gather the trash around our house weekly and take the garbage can out to the road for the pickup every Tuesday. It is also his job to wash the dishes every night after we finish dinner. These are two responsibilities that he has and he

> **"And just like I knew what was required of me, children today need to know what is required of them."**

knows he's responsible for. As stated in the last chapter, as well, my two-year-old daughter is responsible for using the potty instead of using the bathroom in her underwear. At this point, she has pretty much mastered the art of going to the potty; it is second nature for her, and the need for diapers is a thing of the past. Yes, this is a small duty for her, but it is helping to groom her for future jobs that she'll be accountable for.

When I was a young boy, I was responsible for making sure my room was clean, my bed was made, and my toys were picked up after my friends came over to play in my room. Again, these tasks may be minor, but they go a long way in teaching children accountability. And just like I knew what was required of me, children today need to know what is required of them. They need to get to a point where they are not asked to do their task; they already know they need to do it.

Third, it is a parent's duty to help a child **identify positive and negative consequences** for all of their actions. If you make straight A's in school, there is a positive consequence for that. If you get into a fight at school, there will be a negative consequence for that. Participating in community service events will reap a positive benefit. Cursing out your sister or brother will result in something negative. A child needs to understand how important consequences are and what roles they can play in their lives in the long run. I knew that to get into a good college, I needed to work very hard in school. I had my eyes set on attending one of the top tech colleges in the nation, but I understood I would never make it through their doors and be admitted if I didn't work hard in school. The fear of not succeeding pushed me to work hard.

These same set of rules can be applied to the lives of children, teenagers, and even adults. Life is full of consequences and little decisions that can make or break you. Should I buy this $200 purse instead of purchasing my books for school? Is it wise to skip school today and hang at the mall instead? Is this extra credit assignment worth the additional 20 minutes of homework time? Because of the lessons you've been taught throughout your life, making these types of decisions should become easier to make as you progress through your journey.

Last, it is very important for parents to **remain consistent in the accolades and punishments** they give their children. If your child is working hard in school and bringing home great grades, make sure you are consistently rewarding them. If your child keeps disrespecting you in your home, make sure their punishment is consistent every time. Staying consistent in praise and reprimand lets a child know you are serious; it shows them you will not back down from rewarding or punishing them.

Growing up, my mother was always consistent in disciplining me, even when I stood inches above her. I can remember a time when I was around 18 years old and disrespected my mother after coming home late one night. Although I was past the age of spankings and pops on my leg, my mom still recognized the importance of maintaining the rules that I had been taught growing up. She refused to let me get away with breaking one of her rules, and this is the mentality that parents today should uphold when raising their kids. Simply put, your child can never be too old to learn an important life lesson. Momma would send me to go live with someone else before I would disrespect her in our home. That was one thing that she would not tolerate. This is why I loved her so much.

If you learn one thing from this chapter, let it be this: It is important to instill rules and consequences for your children early on in their lives. Doing this will prevent unnecessary heartbreak, debilitating stress, and shouting matches with your child as they grow into adulthood. Discipline from fear may be hard to implement at first, but I can guarantee it will pay off for you and your child in the long run because it creates structure and boundaries that not only will protect your child as he or she grows older, but will also help create a responsible, respectful person.

Chapter 8 – A Woman Can't Raise a Man?

"I was raised by a single mother who made a way for me. She used to scrub floors as a domestic worker, put a cleaning rag in her pocketbook and ride the subways in Brooklyn so I would have food on the table. But she taught me as I walked her to the subway that life is about not where you start, but where you're going."

–Rev. Al Sharpton, Civil Rights Activist

I want to start this chapter with a very important message: Although I talk about growing up without a father and the willpower my mother showed in making sure I was taken care of, I am pro-family. If a mother and father can work through their issues to create a loving and welcoming home for their children, I am in full support of that. A two-parent household is the ideal situation and shouldn't be the exception to the rule.

There is a cliché that many of us have heard and believe to be true: A woman can't raise a man. Some skeptics believe that a boy will miss out on key conversations and life lessons with his mother—how does she talk to him about sex? Will he fear her when he stands a foot taller than her? How will she instill discipline in his life as he branches out into his manhood? Although this saying has some truth to it, it's not the standard by which people should live their lives. I am a living testimony that a woman can raise a boy to become a respectful, God-fearing man that takes care of his responsibilities, raises a family, and creates an empire that makes his family proud.

I am living proof that it can be done.

My mother was a strong woman. As you may have gathered from previous chapters, she owned up to her responsibilities, worked hard every day, and instilled discipline in her son that I could pass on to my children. When my father ceased paying child support when I was 8 years old, she knew it was up to her to support me financially on a full-time basis. A mother's love rises above all others—it knows no boundaries; it remains steadfast when everyone else has walked away.

Throughout history, countless men have recognized the importance of their mother's love and support. Powerful leaders such as U.S. presidents appreciate the love and support given to them by their mothers. Abraham Lincoln said, "I remember my mother's prayers and they have followed me. They have clung to me all my life." George Washington was quoted as saying, "My mother was the most beautiful woman I ever saw. All I am I owe to my mother. I attribute all of my success in life to the moral, intellectual and physical education I received from her." Famed author Ralph Waldo Emerson said, "Men are what their mothers made them."

And I'd have to say that all of these quotes are true.

My mother knew the odds were against her in raising a boy on her own. Unlike a young girl, she couldn't dress me up in baby doll tops and put barrettes in my hair. We couldn't go shopping for new Mary Jane shoes or talk about the people in class I thought were cute. However, she still made an impact in my life. All that I am today, I owe to my mother. I'm successful because of her love, guidance, and support in every aspect of my life.

I'm sure there are women reading this book that feel the pressure behind raising their sons on their own. I know from personal experience that it can sometimes be tricky raising children in a two-parent household—there are times when my wife and I feel slightly overwhelmed with maintaining our professional lives and personal lives and making sure our children have all of the attention they need. I can only imagine how single mothers feel when doing it on their own. Despite the challenges they face when raising their sons, there are key steps in ensuring their sons become productive adults after they leave their mother's daily care.

1. There *always* needs to be a focus on God. Every household needs a spiritual foundation based in God's grace and mercy. There will be times when you feel like you can't go on; everything will seem to overwhelm you, and you'll feel helpless. This is the

time when you *need* God. Don't get me wrong, you should praise His name at all times. However, trusting in the Lord when you are faced with challenges and adversities will help alleviate the stress you have surrounding the upbringing of your children. Proverbs 3:5-6 states, "Trust in the Lord with all your heart and lean not on your own understanding. In all your ways submit to him, and he will make your paths straight." Trust in Him when life seems impossible. Trust in Him when you're all out of options.

Believe in Him like He believes in you.

2. If possible, surround your son with positive male influences that will teach him the difference between right and wrong. Make sure you know what these role models believe in; what they stand for could make or break your son in the long run. Growing up, my

PawPaw and three uncles were the positive males I looked up to when I couldn't have certain conversations with my mother. They'd be the ones I could sit down and talk sports with. They'd give me a man's point of view regarding girls and would always be there to listen to various problems I had in school, on my job, and at home with my mom. They helped shape the way I saw the world. Without them, I realize that rearing me could have become difficult for my mom. They were her backup. She was the general, and they were the soldiers. In this journey called life, you need both at all times.

3. Get your sons involved in a mentorship program, whether that is through sports, a debate team, or a life-skills program, where a male mentor is present. We all know that kids act differently around non-family members. They know they need to be

on their best behavior when momma and auntie are around, but it's important they still know what's appropriate when they're away from home. A male mentor will help guide your child, even during their downtime. For example, many famous athletes, politicians, and leaders can think back to a positive mentor that helped change the direction of their lives. There are countless interviews and documentaries featuring people like retired NBA star Allen Iverson, actor Denzel Washington, and former NFL coach and motivational speaker Tony Dungy who can recall that group of mentors who added that *something* to their lives. Their role models believed in them when they were first starting in their craft, and these famous men still thank them to this day. There's nothing like someone believing in you—it's something a young man will never forget.

I'll end this chapter with a story. During the late 1940s and early 1950s, runner Roger Bannister was on a mission to become the fastest man in the world to run the mile. At the time, he was clocked at hovering just above 4 minutes to run it. Many people believed it would be impossible to run that distance in less than 4 minutes. Think about it—it takes the average person over 8 minutes to jog that distance. Imagine *that* kind of speed!

After a disappointing showing at the 1952 Olympics, Bannister devoted his life to running the mile as fast as possible, preferably under 4 minutes. After one track meet at the University of Oxford in England, Bannister beat competitor Chris Chataway, proving to him "...the 4-minute mile was not out of reach."

On May 6, 1954, Bannister participated in a meet between team British AAA and the University of Oxford Iffley Road Track in England. Bannister, part of British AAA, ran as hard and fast as possible and wound up running the mile in 3 minutes and 59 seconds. The 3,000 spectators of the event erupted in cheers as the announcer declared the new world record, a feat that almost everyone believed to be impossible and unrealistic. Since that was accomplished, more than 50 years later, over 1,000 people have also run the mile under 4 minutes. It took one person to set the pace, and once it was done, others had the confidence that they could do it, too.

The moral of the story is this: Just because people say something can't be done doesn't mean it can't be done. Just because a mass audience believes a mother can't raise a child in a loving and supportive household doesn't make that statement true. Those are merely the opinions of individuals, not the gospel of God. We are all born into different life situations. Some of us may have been surrounded by the love of both parents, whereas others only had a mother or a father to have their back. Regardless, our start in life should not negatively determine our journey. Just as my mother did, all single mothers out there should rest assure that they *can* raise a well-respected and loving man that will pass their lessons and affection to his family one day.

The Fatherless Father

120

Chapter 9 – Getting Rid of the Anger

"Turn your wounds into wisdom."
–Oprah Winfrey

When I was around 12 years old, I would get unimaginably angry when anyone would mention my father or ask me where he was. I had not heard from my father in over a decade, so at 12, anger towards him was at an all-time high. As I've mentioned in earlier chapters, it was hard for me to process how this man who gave me life could ultimately deny my existence by cutting off contact from me and my mother. I believed he was ashamed of me, almost like I was a mistake.

I never really had conversations with my mother about how I felt. She wasn't an emotional woman, and perhaps that was because of the fact that she was raising a son on her own. Maybe she felt that she had to be strong for me and not cry or show any other emotion when I was present. Because of this, talking to her about my anger was kind of out of the question. I don't think she would have dismissed my questions and emotions surrounding my father's disappearance, but she may not have known how to properly address them or started to question whether she was doing a good enough job.

Thus, I had a sort of passive-aggressive mentality when it came to others mentioning my dad. Looking back on it, I understand how unhealthy this was. As a father, I encourage my son to talk to me about his feelings towards certain things because I know how bad not sharing it can be.

Right before I turned 13, I got into a fist fight with this boy named Rusty on my baseball team. Minor fights are not foreign to locker rooms and playing fields because young boys (and even grown men sometimes) want to prove that they are stronger and better than their opponent. It goes back to the competitive nature I described in Chapter 5: as a boy involved in sports, you always want to defeat your opponent, and that is exactly what I did to Rusty. You may wonder, "What did Rusty do to make you lash out and beat up your teammate?" He did the one thing that no one should have done to me.

He brought up my father.

You see, Rusty's dad was the head coach of our baseball team. He always knew where his dad was and even got to spend time with him during practice and at games, privileges I was not afforded with my father. One day, Rusty decided to bring up my dad and point out the fact that he was gone from my life and was never coming back. The anger I kept so well-hidden inside of me came out in a mad explosion of emotions, and I proceeded to tackle him to the ground and beat his face into a bloody mess. I was angry and I wasn't taking his taunting anymore.

Needless to say, I was almost kicked off the team because of my actions. I now realize how my anger towards my teammate was really directed at the pain and hurt I felt towards my father for leaving me. If Rusty had said something about my mother's hair being messy or my grades being poor, I probably would have ignored him because those things weren't true. This is a key point to remember: The things that hurt us the most usually stem from beliefs and opinions we secretly struggle with.

There were other times throughout my childhood where I grew angry at my father, but most of these emotions were internalized. I know there are many young men walking around right now who feel the same way—they are confused about their relationship with their father (or the lack thereof) but don't have anyone to talk to about what they're dealing with. Reflecting on my past, I wish I'd had someone I could open up to about my resentment towards my father. I'm sure my uncles and grandfather would have been open to discussing the topic, but there were times when I felt a young man was strong when he didn't show that vulnerable side of himself. Perhaps some young boy reading this book right now feels the same way.

Anger is a very powerful emotion to have, especially if it makes you act out in negative ways. Look at all the young men currently serving time in prison for violent crimes. Observe the behavior of young boys that feel it's OK to curse at their teachers or be disrespectful to the older woman on the train and to even their own mothers. One has to wonder what kind of anger, sadness, or anxiety they are dealing with to commit the nasty acts they participate in. Anger can lead someone to regret a choice they've made; it can make them regret saying a hurtful thing to a family member or loved one. Unfortunately, it can break seemingly steady and loving relationships with a few cutting words and irreversible actions.

So what can be done to prevent a young man from falling into the dangerous world of hiding his fury? How can parents and loved ones reach a young boy and show him it's OK to feel the emotions he's experiencing?

You let him know that you're there with an open ear early in his life.

As a parent, it is your responsibility to pay attention to any abnormal behavior your child displays. Don't overlook the concern his teacher discusses with you regarding his aggressiveness toward his classmates on the playground. Do not dismiss the fist fights he is getting into with his siblings at home. It is important to nip this behavior in the bud as soon as possible—if you consider it as a "boy being a boy" thing, you may live to regret it once he's older and you're unable to control his behavior.

Once you're able to pinpoint the origin of his

> **"Once you're able to pinpoint the origin of his anger, you can map out ways to address the issue."**

anger, you can map out ways to address the issue. As mentioned in the previous chapter, find a positive male role model your son can look up to in a father-like way. Of course, the coach or teacher or mentor can't take the place of the man who helped give your son life, but he can assist in giving your son the critical things he needs to survive this world: Acceptance. Focus. Recognition.

In the end, there are countless things that can prompt a young man to harbor negative feelings, which may result in behavior problems later in life. However, it is my mission to help young men around the world understand that keeping quiet about their internal conflicts is not only unhealthy, but could also lead to adverse consequences. I implore parents to keep their children uplifted and show them that they are not on this life journey alone—they have you, someone always willing and able to help them navigate their emotions and find a positive way of dealing with them.

The Fatherless Father

Chapter 10 – Breaking the Generational Curse

"A man can be as great as he wants to be. If you believe in yourself and have the courage, the determination, the dedication, the competitive drive, and if you are willing to sacrifice the little things in life and pay the price for the things that are worthwhile, it can be done."

–Maya Angelou, poet and award-winning author

Bad habits are hard to break.

We all have at least one. Some people have a hard time being responsible with their money. Others take personal relationships for granted by always thinking their loved ones will be there. Additionally, there are those who are quick to anger, and they completely disregard the consequences they'll face if they physically or emotionally harm another. Finally, there

129

are those who don't eat healthy and nutritious foods and always choose to eat at fast food restaurants and consume foods high in fat, cholesterol, and sodium.

Many people believe that most of the habits we have are learned early on in our lives. So much research has been done linking the importance of a positive, safe childhood to a positive and safe adulthood. At the end of the day, many of the decision-making abilities surrounding our lives are learned from our parents. For example, I understand how important my mother's teachings on education were in shaping the direction of my life. Without these lessons, I'm not sure I would be the successful entrepreneur, community activist, and father I am today. As a man, I see how vital it is to pave my own path, but I recognize that nothing would be possible if it had not been for my mother's guidance.

Simply put, I was loved.

However, I recognize that there are numerous young people in the world who don't have the type of love, discipline, and structure my mother added to my life. There are children all over the world who are growing up in parentless homes. There are kids who are dealing with parents who are alcoholics, drug addicts, or focus more on their current boyfriend or girlfriend instead of acknowledging that their child's welfare comes above all others. And, unfortunately, there are young people who have parents who are unconcerned with their children's lives. At the end of the day, these parents don't really care what kind of right or wrong decisions their child makes as long as they're not bothered by them. It can be argued that when a child grows up in a household like the ones described above, they fear they will end up being exactly like their parent.

Let's look further at this false belief for a moment. How many people, both young and old, are dreadfully afraid they are going to become or are starting to act like their parents? Do you know someone who thinks it's guaranteed that they'll become their parents, participating in the destructive behaviors they witnessed when they came home from school? Countless individuals honestly believe that "because my parents were this way, that's the way I'm going to be." What's even worse is they don't even try to fight this terrible mindset. They just take it as their expected destiny and live their lives accordingly. In short, they have no motivation of breaking this generational curse that seems to plague their family.

Generational curses are tough in nature and harmful to one's livelihood. This is primarily caused by the disbelief that there are other options and choices to be made, breaking away from the ones that were made in the past. For example, there are countless families where the great-grandmother, grandmother, mother, and daughter were all single parents. Certain families believe that because they've always lived in the projects, that's just the way things are—in their mind, there is "no way" this will ever change (although this couldn't be further from the truth). Some people saw how alcoholism crushed the life of a parent, and they are petrified that they will face the same challenge. In all these situations, they honestly feel that they are trapped in this world, and they'll never be able to break away from it.

I'll admit the generational curse of being a fatherless father who wouldn't play an active role in his child's life crossed my mind when I was younger. As I mentioned in previous chapters, I dealt with moments of anger, confusion, and frustration surrounding my father's disappearance from my life. (I found out later in my life that my father grew up without his father, so my fear of inheriting the "fatherless" role haunted me.) The last thing I wanted to do was have a child one day and not be active in his or her life. I made the decision to step up, especially the first time I found out I was going to be father. I saw firsthand growing up how much it hurt me to not see my dad at my first baseball game or when I graduated in the top of my high school class. How I wish he could have been there when I opened my acceptance letter for college and when I started my first major job at Georgia Power. Those were all milestones I wished he was there for; they were also moments I knew I wouldn't miss when my children experienced them in their lifetimes.

Some of you may be reading this chapter thinking, "Reco, it's not that simple. Breaking the generational curse in my family is hard, especially when my grandparents, parents, siblings, and extended family members all hold the same negative, destructive belief and participate in certain behaviors." To this statement, I would agree. It's not that simple.

Breaking a habit or behavior is an extremely hard thing to do. Ask the person who is 7 years sober from alcohol if it's ever easy to walk away from something that became a daily part of their lives. Find a recovering shopaholic and ask whether or not financial responsibility is easy for them. They'd much rather go to their local mall and spend $800 on shoes, clothes, and useless accessories instead of using the money to pay their living expenses. Breaking these unconscious behavioral patterns are huge obstacles; however, they can be done.

When breaking a generational curse or habit, one must first recognize the negative trait and come up with several solutions to the problem. To illustrate, let's look at a common challenge in various communities in America: single-parent households run solely by the mother. Her kids may feel they are doomed to be like their struggling mother—overwhelmed, financially-stressed, and frustrated with her level of mobility in life, which is due to having several children to take care of on their own. As parents, we should always encourage our children to strive beyond what we did or did not accomplish in our lifetime. I would tell her children that their mother's life doesn't have to be their destiny. They have a choice to make different decisions that could lead to them eventually becoming the same age but childless, in school, and taking the proper steps to live a rewarding life.

I look back to the lessons my mother taught me while I grew up. Without fail, she repeated over and over to me how important my education was; it would be the solution to many struggles I could have potentially faced as an adult. She would not allow my lack of a father to cripple me from success; she pushed me to focus academically and supplied me with the proper tools to be successful in life. Again, she would not allow her issues as an adult to affect me as a young boy.

The next step to breaking the cycle is to surround yourself with likeminded people who desire the same things you want in life. Let's refer back to Will Smith's quote, "You can tell how far in life you'll go by the five people you spend the most amount of time with." I cannot emphasize enough how crucial it is to spend time with likeminded people who want to break away from negative family traits and make something better of their life. Young people, instead of always being concerned with dating and who's cute, which could potentially lead to a bad and life-changing decision in the form of an unwanted pregnancy, should spend time with other students who are working on college applications, are a part of the student council, and focus more on their grades and test scores as opposed to what Mike and Karen wore to school that day. It may be difficult, but try to take your focus away from the negative things that go on at home and at school and put your energy and heart into your school work, part-time job, new business idea, or positive relationships that will benefit your life years from now.

Finally, do not obsess about whether or not you're becoming like your parents. **Focus on who you are becoming as an individual**. It doesn't make sense to panic and forfeit the chance at having a meaningful life free from financial worries, anger, and oppression. It *does* make sense to take each day as it comes and worry only about which direction you're taking *your* life. In the end, your motivation for change should center directly on desiring a better life for you and your potential family one day.

In conclusion, a negative generational trait is tough to overcome. I have firsthand experience. Again, I made a decision that I was not going to be afraid of continuing the generational curse, but instead, I made a decision early on that I was going to break this curse. It is important to understand that we all must recognize the curse exists, decide to break it, and take action that begins the curse destruction process. Always remember, you cannot correct what you are not willing to confront. These are the first steps in creating a more gratifying and worthwhile life for yourself and future generations.

The Fatherless Father

Chapter 11 – Fatherless National Epidemic

"I cannot think of any need in childhood as strong as the need for a father's protection."
–Sigmund Freud, neurologist and psychoanalyst

As you may have picked up from the previous chapters, this book surrounds the challenges faced when a child grows up in a fatherless home. My mother did the best job she could raising me, her only child, on her own. I can only imagine the struggles faced by mothers responsible for a handful of kids who do it on their own. Yet, with this chapter, I wanted to present statistical proof that shows how a fatherless home can negatively change the way a child sees themselves and the world. By the time you, especially the fathers reading these words, get to the final paragraph, I want you to understand how the fatherless household epidemic really *does* matter in the development of your child, whether they're a young man or a young lady. This chapter will focus less on my own personal experiences and more on real statistics and facts that have been gathered over the years.

First, the imprisonment rates of people that grew up in fatherless homes are astronomically high. In a 2004 issue of the *Journal of Research on Adolescence*, authors Cynthia Harper of the University of Pennsylvania and Sara S. McLanahan found that "Young men who grow up in homes without fathers are twice as likely to end up in jail as those who come from traditional two-parent families... those boys whose fathers were absent from the household had double the odds of being incarcerated, even when other factors such as race, income, parent education and urban residence were held constant." Take a moment to think about that. A young man, regardless of his race, household income, or where he lives, is twice as likely to end up in jail as a young man who had both parents in his home. Although this statistic isn't the outcome of every young man in a fatherless home, that statistic is overwhelmingly depressing. It's something to think about; many of the men in prison today may not have been there if their father had accepted his responsibility and made the decision to be a part of his child's life.

Next, research from the article "What Can the Federal Government Do to Decrease Crime and Revitalize Communities?" published by the National Institute of Justice, found that "85% of all children that exhibit behavioral disorders come from fatherless homes." In other words, children who have anger issues, who get into fights at school, and have behavior problems in the classroom and at home come from a home where the father is not there. Imagine how much that number could significantly decrease if a father took responsibility, worked things out with the child's mom, and played an active role in the lives of these kids. Conversely, if the child's mother took responsibility and was willing to work things out with the father and allow him to play a more active role in the lives of these kids, this outcome could be different.

This same article also found that "a little more than 70% of all high school dropouts come from fatherless homes." Imagine all of the potential neurosurgeons, lawyers, teachers, and businesspersons that could have been but will never be, stemming from the complications surrounding growing up in a fatherless home. For boys and girls, high school can be a very challenging time. There's the anxiety surrounding keeping up with classes, fitting in to the "right" crowd, working a part-time job, avoiding the recruitment of being in a gang, and finding yourself. Put all of those things together and add in a fatherless household, and you get a child that has the weight of the world on their shoulders.

Additionally, this article states that "70% of juveniles in state-operated institutions come from fatherless homes." If the child is a minor in a youth detention center, he or she is just one step away from landing in a more permanent facility, such as an adult correctional facility. Like the previous three statistics, this tragic percentage could be reduced considerably if a father was active in the life of his children.

Next, aggression in a child growing up in a fatherless home is drastically higher than in a child who comes from a two-parent household. In the *Journal of Abnormal Children* article entitled "Household Family Structure and Children's

Aggressive Behavior: A Longitudinal Study of Urban Elementary School Children," researchers N. Vaden-Kierman, N. Ialongo, J. Pearson, and S. Kellman found a very disturbing statistic. After studying approximately 1,200 fourth-grade students, they discovered "greater levels of aggression in boys from mother-only households than from boys in mother-father households." This discovery is something I can most certainly connect with (as explained in Chapter 4 – "Getting Rid of the Anger"). When I was younger, I was angry. I fought people who mentioned my father. I couldn't understand why I had all of this anger surrounding my mental processes and behavior at school and with my friends. Now, as a man, I know and understand why. My aggressive behavior was, in part, because of missing my father and the jealousy I felt for the boys my age who were blessed enough to have their dads supporting them with their academics, attending their sporting events, and always being a solid voice of reason in an uncertain world.

Finally, the United States Department of Health and Human Services found that "90% of homeless and runaway children are from fatherless homes." Teenage homelessness is a major problem in the

United States. How much could this problem be solved if fathers played a positive role in these kids' lives?

Still not convinced that the fatherless household impacts a child's life? Here's a shocking statistic: According to the website *The Fatherless Generation*, young girls growing up in a fatherless household have an extreme uphill battle to face. The website reports that "Daughters of single parents without a father involved are 53% more likely to marry as teenagers, 711% more likely to have children as teenagers, 164% more likely to have a pre-marital birth, and 92% more likely to get divorced themselves."[1] Let's break these numbers down. One out of every two girls who grow up in a fatherless home are more likely to get married before the age of 20. At this age, a child should be focusing on their sophomore college English class instead of where their wedding will be held. It is absolutely mind-blowing that a girl without a father is over 700% more likely to start having kids as a

---

[1] *The Fatherless Generation.*
http://thefatherlessgeneration.wordpress.com/statistics/ (Oct 2012)

teenager. Without her father present in her life, she may seek the comfort of another male, which could lead to not saying no to sexual pressure for the fear of losing another male presence in her life. The vast majority of these young girls are not prepared for the life-changing consequences they will face after deciding to have sex. Although this book focuses a great deal on the challenges faced by single mothers when raising young men, it is equally important to realize how much of a negative impact a fatherless household can have on the life of a young woman. It should be every parent's intent to make sure his or her child has a rewarding childhood. It should be their mission to ensure they're playing a disciplinary role in the lives of their children.

Let's look at things from the opposite perspective. I want to illustrate the positive impact a two-parent home has in the lives of children. *The Fatherless Generation* site also found:

- Children with fathers who are involved are 40% less likely to repeat a grade in school.
- Children with fathers who are involved are 70% less likely to drop out of school.

- Children with fathers who are involved are more likely to get A's in school.
- Children with fathers who are involved are more likely to enjoy school and engage in extracurricular activities.

Simply stated, being a father matters. Being an active father matters more. But being an active father who lives at home with his children, supports them academically, financially, socially, and spiritually matters *most*. I know there are many individuals out there who say a mother's love cannot be topped, and they may have a point. However, a father's presence should not be dismissed or deemed less important. Fathers matter.

I understand that many women and men have complicated relationships; it's not as simple as forgive, forget, and raise your kids. Some men and women simply no longer get along with each other. Some folks used to date in high school and college, had a child, and then grew in different directions. I understand those types of circumstances. However, with the exception of fathers who have been taken out of their children's lives by death, mothers and fathers

146

should both make an attempt to be present. The guidance and structure set by a parent is second to none. It sets the tone for the type of life their child will live. The responsibility cannot be placed solely on the mother. Fathers should also be able to step up to the plate and engage with their child. It's important for couples who are no longer together to realize that it's no longer just about the two of them: The livelihood of their children matter more than the issues the two of them have with each other.

If the father is unwilling to take part in his offspring's life, family members should find another positive male who will take on the father-like role for the child. The statistics mentioned in this chapter are proof that it makes all the difference. It is important to note that this man should enter the child's life at a very early age, especially because this is the time when behaviors and attitudes are learned and engrained into a child's mind.

At the end of the day, a child may or may not say they miss their father. They may be like the young boy in Chapter 1 who asked, "Mommy, how come I never see my dad?" They may be like Dennis Rodman or

Howard Stern, two popular entertainers, who have lived alternative lifestyles filled with run-ins with the law, dressing like drag queens, and behaving outlandishly, which they both partially blame on the absence of their fathers. Additionally, the youngster could have a childhood like singer Nicki Minaj, who for years witnessed her father battle with alcohol and drug abuse, as well as be a violent man towards her mother. Perhaps her current persona stems from the trauma she witnessed as a child.

On the opposite side, the juvenile could be like billionaire and media mogul Oprah Winfrey, a victim of physical and sexual abuse and a lost pregnancy but still fought for her success and didn't use her past as a roadblock to it. Or the child may be like me—a young boy who bottles up his emotions surrounding his father's inactive role in his life so the anger and frustration is taken out on the first person who makes fun of them or teases them. Finally, they could be one of the many negative statistics described in this chapter. Regardless of their financial situation, their ethnicity, or household education level, a dad's role is imperative from the time a child is born until they are an adult. Believe me, a person will never forget the feelings they had as a young child, dreaming that their dad will open the front door and say, "I'm home."

The Fatherless Father

Chapter 12 – Becoming a Fatherless Father

"Everything you can imagine is real."
—Pablo Picasso

How does a mother prepare herself to have a talk with her son about the birds and the bees? As a single parent, does she wonder whether she's the right person to have the talk with him, worrying that she won't know what to say and whether or not her son will take her advice to heart? My mother never had the conversation with me, although looking back on it, I wish she had. The thought of her sitting down saying, "Reco, lemme talk to you about how two people make a baby," would have been really uncomfortable when I was 14 years old. Knowing me, I would have turned and walked out of the room, not knowing what she was going to say! Sometimes, southern mothers keep it a little too real and their kids can't handle it! I wasn't afraid, but I don't think I could have had that conversation with my mother.

When a parent doesn't teach a child about sex at the appropriate age, they leave their offspring open to learn about the subject from improper sources: friends, TV, magazines, the internet, and other forms of media. What mother would want her child to learn about the subject from a women's magazine at the check-out line at the grocery store? What father would want his daughter to learn about relationships and sex from watching an episode of *Basketball Wives*, *The Real Housewives of Atlanta,* or *Grey's Anatomy*? Furthermore, with the age of the internet, would any parent want their child to learn about sex from an inappropriate website that shows the pleasure behind the act but not the potential consequences?

My experiences of learning about the birds and the bees started early in my life because my uncles took it upon themselves to fill me in on what they felt I needed to know. My oldest uncle would leave adult magazines on the coffee table and pornographic video tapes near the VCR. Can you imagine a 13-year-old boy consuming that kind of material at such a young age? I sure appreciated it when I was younger, but now I understand that this was probably not the correct way to inform me about women and sex.

My youngest uncle would have conversations with his friends about his "adventures" with women in front of me, not knowing that I was paying serious attention. I would also overhear his activities he participated in with his girlfriend when I sometimes spent the night at his apartment. Being surrounded by these types of events was exciting for me at the time; it was also detrimental in painting a false picture of the link between sex and pregnancy.

Needless to say, I was intrigued by the idea of sex as I grew older. I never had conversations with my mother about it, and I had no father around to discuss my thoughts, feelings, and questions surrounding the act, so I was kind of in a learn-as-you-go mentality. I took what I knew and my experiences around the act and shared it with my friends—this is how I formed my opinions and views about the birds and the bees. It's ironic, however, that I placed a spotlight on the act of sex but not the aftermath or consequences that could stem from sex with a girl. Those pornographic videos that my uncle left out didn't have a girl taking a pregnancy test a few weeks after she was intimate with her co-star. There are no adult magazines that have Miss October standing in a center-page spread posing during the eighth month of her pregnancy with a caption beneath saying, "This could be your baby!" No, these immediate consequences are not brought to the attention of young boys like me growing up. With the internet creating yet another gateway for young boys to have access to sexual topics and acts, it's even easier for them to learn about how great sex can be, but not about the repercussions that can come from it. For many young men, myself included, there's only one question on our minds.

What's the worst that can happen?

I had this mentality in my late teenage years as I finished up high school and went off to college. I was feeling pretty good: I had great grades, and I was accepted into one of the top tech universities in the country. I had a plan. I had determination. I had drive. I dated a few girls here and there in high school but wasn't trying to start up anything too serious right before I started college. I didn't want to drag commitment from one place to another. I was just looking to have fun while I moved forward to being successful in life.

Right before I started my dual-degree program in Physics and Electrical Engineering at the State University of West Georgia and Georgia Tech, I met this young lady that I went out with, but in reality, it was really just puppy love—a good time and another experience for me to have. I was more focused on working on my academics, looking for employment, and partying! It's important to note that the State University of West Georgia was a huge party school at the time, so I was doing my work and keeping my focus during the day, whereas I kicked it at parties and lived the good life in the evenings and weekends. Then, right before my first semester ended, I started to interview for a rotational co-op student position at several companies in Georgia—this is where a college student would be hired by a company to start working in the field their degree was in to get college credit and also gain experience. Shortly after meeting with various companies, I was hired by the Southern Company as a co-op design engineer for their largest subsidiary, Georgia Power. Typically, the company would only hire students that were at least in their second year, but I was hired early because they were impressed by my hunger for learning more about the industry, my potential, and my promise. The human resources manager later told me that I was one of those young people that a company could look at and say, "That young man is going to be something special. He just has that 'it' factor!"

At this point, my focus was on school work, my rotational co-op, and all of the benefits that came from working and making $20 an hour. I was able to put nice chrome rims on my car, buy nice polo shirts, go to the movies whenever I wanted, and even go so far as save money for a nice Spring Break trip. I had it all planned out! I felt like I was the man and that nothing could possibly go wrong in my life.

Then, I got the call.

I noticed how shaky her voice was on the phone. At first, I tried to dismiss the nervousness I heard in her voice, but in my gut, I knew something was wrong.

"Hey, Reco, can I talk to you?" she said.

"Yea, girl, what's up?"

"Ummm... something came up," she said in a vague and anxious tone.

"OK? Girl, what's wrong with you? Why you actin' so funny?"

"Are you sitting down?"

"No, I just got in from class. WHAT IS GOING ON?!? Tell me what has happened," I breathlessly said in response.

"Reco, I may be pregnant."

Silence.

More silence.

Panic.

Fear.

Confusion.

Did she say what I think she just said? How is this possible? Why wasn't I more careful? What am I gonna do?!?

"Reco, did you hear me? Say something," she said.

At this point, I felt like my world was closing up. My breathing quickened to a point where I felt there was no oxygen left in the room. I was pretty sure my heart would beat all the way out of my chest. I lost the feeling in my legs. My palms were so sweaty that I almost dropped the phone onto the floor.

"Uhhh... yea, I heard you. Are you sure?" I said in a near whisper.

"I think so. My period was supposed to be here about 2 weeks ago and it hasn't come," she responded.

At this point, pure terror started to slowly creep in. I kept wondering, *Is she sure? Is she sure? Is she sure?* My mind would not allow me to fully believe that this girl could be pregnant. Reflecting on this, I was in denial about what was going down because I was so fearful about losing the lifestyle I was just starting to get used to with school and the new job. I just didn't want this news to be true. I made the decision that night that I'd go home the next week and see if this girl was really pregnant. I wasn't sure what her motives could be, so I needed to determine beyond a shadow of a doubt that her news was really real.

Shortly after this conversation, I went home the next weekend to meet with her. As long as I live, I will never forget the scared feeling I had when I walked through the pharmacy doors with her to buy a box of two pregnancy tests. I needed to get two to confirm whether the first test read the same results as the other. Since my mother was not home that evening, we decided that we'd skip the movies and take the pregnancy tests.

I was pretty confident that she wasn't going to be pregnant because something like this couldn't happen to me. I'm sure many guys my age felt the same way when their girls told them they were pregnant—*this cannot be happening to me*! But for me, that mentality was ringing loud in my mind—*THIS CANNOT BE HAPPENING TO ME!*

We went through the instructions on the box line by line and read it very slowly. I wanted to make sure we understood the process.

"You ready?" she asked me.

"Yea, let's just get this over with," I responded.

Shortly after reading and giving me a brief glance, she went into the bathroom to take the test. Even though I was confident that she wouldn't be pregnant, those 2 minutes seemed like the longest 2 minutes of my life! I paced back and forth in the living room, praying that she would come out with negative pregnancy tests. It was one of those moments where I promised I'd never be reckless again if it turned out I wouldn't be a father. I just needed to get a second chance.

That second chance would never come.

When she opened the door to that bathroom, everything seemed to happen in slow motion. She rounded the corner and walked into the living room with tears in her eyes and the look that it was true.

She really was pregnant.

"No! No! It can't be true!" I frantically said to her.

She couldn't even speak. At a loss for words, she handed me the sticks, and I saw for myself—they were both positive. I was going to be a father.

We both walked over to the couch and sat down, stunned. We stared off in space, both with panicked looks on our faces, realizing that our lives would forever be changed. After 30 minutes of stunned silence, I decided I needed to be a man and speak up about what the next steps were.

"We should probably tell our parents," I weakly said. Ironically, she was raised by and lived with her grandmother, as her mother passed away when she was a toddler.

"Yes, but how?" she responded. "They are gonna kill us! What have we done?" she cried.

Although I held in my emotions pretty well, I wanted to cry, too. I wanted to cry for making poor decisions. I wanted to cry because I knew my mother would be terribly disappointed and upset with me. But mainly, I wanted to cry because I knew I made a poor decision that could either make or break my life. I always had a plan, a mode of attack, but right then, I didn't know what we were going to do.

After trying to come up with various game plans, nothing sounded like it would work. I didn't have the courage to tell my mother, and she was afraid to tell her grandmother, so we decided we wouldn't say anything to them until it was necessary. With that decision, I went back to school after the weekend was over and tried to go back to life as normal. I soon found out this would be easier said than done.

When I got back to school, I could not focus at all. I would daze off in my classes thinking about the news I had just learned. I had sleepless nights, and my stomach churned each time I thought about being a father in less than a year! *What am I gonna do? Am I ready for this?* As stressed out as I'd become, she was going through far worse things, one being night sickness. I heard briefly somewhere in my past about morning sickness but never night sickness, so I immediately began to panic! I didn't want anything to harm the baby, and not being certain of whether night sickness was a good or bad thing, we decided that we should probably get her in to see a doctor to advise her on the pregnancy. In the meantime, I felt like I needed to tell a family member about what was going on with me, so I called my Auntie Paulette one early Saturday morning and asked if she wanted to go for a drive. She agreed. I went to pick her up and felt completely anxious and freaked out about having to share my actions with her. After about an hour of driving around, I told her.

"Auntie, I've got something to tell you."

"OK, what's going on? You've been acting funny this entire ride. You OK?"

"No, I'm not. I just found out some news a few weekends ago... my girlfriend is pregnant."

"She's what?!" my aunt asked in a hurry.

"She's pregnant. It's true. We took two pregnancy tests and both came back positive. I'm going to be a daddy."

Brief silence.

"Does your momma know?" she inquired.

"No, not yet. I'm afraid to tell her," I said weakly.

For a moment, Auntie Paulette just sat there in silence, digesting the information I just shared with her. After a couple of minutes, she looked at me and said something that would completely change my life.

"Reco, it's gonna be OK. You'll be alright."

From there, she and I talked about how important it would be for both my girlfriend and I to keep calm and focus on school. She, too, was an advocate for education, so she didn't want us to get off track any more than we already were by the pregnancy. She wanted us to stay in school and keep our eyes to the future while we dealt with this challenge. The thing she was most concerned about was how my mother would kill me once she found out!

Shortly after this meeting with my aunt, I found the courage to tell my mother about what happened. I went home the next weekend and told her about the pregnancy. Although she wasn't completely angry, she was definitely disappointed in me. My mother had always taught me that if I made mistakes or had a mishap, I would have to deal with it accordingly. In fact, one of her favorite sayings was, "You made your bed, now you have to lay in it." This was definitely a time where I'd have to be a man and own up to my responsibilities. I made the decision that I'd be active in my son's life, knowing it was the right thing to do. I knew how hard it was on me to not have my father in my life. I just didn't have it in me to do that to someone else, no matter what kind of future plans I had for myself. Because my father had never been present in my life, I made up my mind that I'd be the greatest dad in the world to my child, something I yearned for ever since I was a young child. I was determined to make up for my hurt and fill my child's life with nothing but joy.

Months went by and there was so much to learn. I found out that my girlfriend was going to have my son, something I was tremendously happy about. *At last, I'll get to do the things with my son that my dad never did with me.* I remember saying that to myself. After my son was born and I held him in my arms for the first time, I experienced a feeling that I really can't explain. At that moment, my perspective on life changed. I knew at that point that all the decisions I made, the actions I took, and the habits I possessed not only affected me, but they also affected this little person that was now depending on me for life.

Numerous people who know me now are somewhat surprised when I say that I owe my son a ton of the credit surrounding my success in life. His birth forced me to become responsible and get serious about life and my future. It's important to remember that some of life's most important lessons are the ones we learn the hard way. My son's birth was a lesson that no matter what obstacle life throws at you, it doesn't mean you throw your hands up and give up. God has willed all of us with the tools we need to push past challenges and move forward with our lives. I used his birth as a stepping stone for something great that would happen to me 10 years later in an event that would change my life even more than his birth.

Chapter 13 – The Importance of Family

"You don't choose your family. They are God's gift to you, as you are to them."
–Bishop Desmond Tutu, social rights activist

Many people underestimate the importance that family can play in their lives. Some believe they've come to be the way they are on their own accord, and no outside influences have played a part in their personality or their character. However, this couldn't be further from the truth. Our immediate family members—mom, dad, and siblings—significantly impact the way we see the world. They shape our beliefs, influence our behavior, and set us up with a list of morals we carry for the rest of our lives. In my case, however, I did not have anyone in my immediate family other than my mother, so it could have been quite easy for me to fall into a world of self-destruction and failure.

There are numerous young people in the world right now that have no positive role models in their lives. They may not know their father or their mother, been abandoned at an early age, or have disengaged family members who do not care about their well-being or their livelihood. I can only imagine how tough it can be growing up in a world where it feels like you don't matter—a place where there is no hope and your world is surrounded in darkness, with no light to be seen or had. It is easy to see how people who grow up like this are often lost and have a negative perception of family and the world that surrounds them. Think about it: If a child has never seen a man and a woman have a successful relationship, where they show love toward each other and their children, how can that child reasonably grow up knowing how to express that love to a potential life partner as an adult? How will they know how to work through their marital issues if they've never seen it done in real life?

I could have easily used my growing up without a father as a defense for not being an active father to my two children. I could have said to myself, *Why should I try to be there for my kids and be open to learning*

168

what a father should do if I never had a man in my life to do that for me? In all honesty, if I had taken that approach—if I had justified my absence from my kids' lives because that was done to me—I would have

> **"Although I didn't actively see a man and a woman together on a regular basis in my own household, I was able to look to my grandparents as the pinnacle of love."**

cowered away from my responsibilities as a father *and* as a man. Being the leading man in a child's life is never easy, whether or not you grew up with a dad. A child should not suffer because a man does not feel he is strong enough to raise his kids, or because he's not sure he has the ability to positively influence the child's life. Being a complete family unit is something that should be expected in a child's life and not seen as the exception.

Looking back on my life, I owe all that I am to my mother and to my extended family members, who were willing to take the spot of my absent father. They showed me that I should never let an absent father handicap me from reaching my full potential. I think about my mother's parents and the love they showed me when I was a rambunctious child, a young father, and an ambitious entrepreneur and motivational speaker later on in my life. They never loved me less when I tripped and made mistakes in my life. They never openly judged me and belittled me when I did things they didn't 100% approve of. They showered me with love, and this is something I'll always admire and love about them. PawPaw would oftentimes sit me down and have one-on-one talks with me about God, life, and how much potential I had. In all honesty, he filled in the open gaps my father left in my life, and for that, I am forever grateful. My grandmother's undying love for me was second to the love my momma gave me growing up. She was the rock that kept my entire family together! You match a phenomenal woman like that with a man who unselfishly showed me grace and mercy, and you can see why I value the input they've had in my life.

Although I didn't actively see a man and a woman together on a regular basis in my own household, I was able to look to my grandparents as the pinnacle of love. It's important to note that they have been married for more than 54 years! Those two people have been through so much together; there's probably been many good times and some bad times, yet they probably wouldn't have it any other way. They are the prime example that has shown me how important it is to work through difficulties with your spouse, and the lessons I learned from them are used currently in my own marriage.

My other extended family members—my aunts and uncles on my mother's side—were also there to help rear me and mold me in to the man I am today. As mentioned in Chapter 4 – "Making it Through Childhood," these family members were a foundation in my life and helped me grow from a boy to a man. My uncles addressed issues that I was uncomfortable bringing up with Momma. My aunt was able to guide me during a challenging time when I was a freshman in college. Many single mothers that are reading this book should understand and realize that having this support system in their children's life *does* matter and *can* help alleviate some of the pressures that come with parenting.

If you leave this chapter with nothing else, it's crucial to remember that any kind of positive love and guidance from extended family members can make all the difference in a child's life. Their love showed me how to love when it was my turn to raise my children. Actor David Ogden Stiers phrased it best, "Family means no one gets left behind or forgotten." It's safe to say my family lived and ruled by this motto, and we are all better for it.

Chapter 14 – The Day Everything Changes

"Bottom line is, even if you see 'em coming, you're not ready for the big moments. No one asks for their life to change, not really. But it does. So what are we, helpless? Puppets? No. The big moments are gonna come. You can't help that. It's what you do afterwards that counts. That's when you find out who you are."

—Joss Whedon, actor and screenwriter

If you ask any person that has achieved great things in their life, they would tell you that it wasn't all smooth sailing to get to their destination. They would share with you the bumps in the road they experienced; they'd envision all of the trials and tribulations they had to overcome in order to come out victorious. When people come out of a low point in life, typically, that moment is their turning point—a time when they make a clear decision that from that moment on, their life will never be the same again. They decide to cut all ties of bondage that are holding them in the past, paralyzed and defeated, to be released into the vision they have for themselves that is waiting with happiness and prosperity. Some make the decision to change at 18 years old, some make it at 80 years old, and some never make the decision at all. But rest assured, when the individual makes the decision, it is the day that everything changes.

Many people have these stories that become defining moments in their life. A decision or some random event happened out of nowhere that changed their perspective on their life moving forward. Or something transpired that disrupted their present, uncovered the past, and undoubtedly transformed their future. Whatever this event or day is called, it came for me at the end of 2010, a moment I will never, ever forget. But first, we must go back a year before this moment to see where this journey began.

On a cool evening in December 2009, Reco Jr. and I were on our way home from his basketball practice. He then asked me a simple yet complex question.

Chapter 14 – The Day Everything Changes

"Daddy, where's your daddy?" he inquired.

Stunned, I looked at him with a puzzling look on my face. *Why is this boy asking me a question like this?*

"Why do you want to know this, son?" I immediately asked him, unsure yet anxious for his answer.

"I want to know because I want to see him. I've never seen him my entire life, and I want to see my granddaddy," he said. "Do you know where he is? Have you talked to him?"

"Junior, I only know what city he lives in, but I don't know where he is," I replied.

"Well, maybe you can find him! I want to know if I have cousins! I want to meet my aunts and uncles. You think I have them? You think my granddaddy has a family for me to meet?"

"I don't know, Junior. I don't know. Maybe I can find out."

My son's question shook me up for two reasons: First, I was unsure of the root reason he asked me this complex question. Did he have the same emotions surrounding not knowing an important family member like I did when I was a young boy? Was he bottling up any anger or resentment inside of him like I did and wasn't telling me? Was this his way of expressing his frustration? Second, I was thrown off due to the fact that I had never really thought about this man since I was 13 years old. That was the age I decided I *never* wanted to see this man or hear about him ever again! Yet, here was my 8-year-old son asking me a question that I was afraid to ask myself, "Where is your daddy?"

After I heard the curiosity and sincerity in my son's voice, I considered my feelings toward my father to be selfish and based in anger. I made a decision that I'd try to find out more information about my father and his side of the family during 2010 so I could answer my son's inquiry and finally close an unanswered chapter in my life's journey.

Little did I know that the information I'd soon find out would turn my world upside down.

176

There were a few things I was told about my father from my mother when I was younger. Charlie McDaniel's father didn't really play an active role in his life growing up. His father had a problem with alcoholism and drifted in and out of his life whenever he felt like it. I also knew that my mother and father were high school sweethearts. Their relationship had its challenges, but Momma loved him. I knew that my mother getting pregnant with me wasn't something he was thrilled about, but he signed my birth certificate and was in and out of my life up until I was 2 years old. Then, suddenly, he disappeared.

I didn't know much more than that, but I figured there was a possibility that there could have been more to the story. As a young boy, I never considered anything besides the story I was told, but as an adult, I understood that there is always two sides to a story.

Although I hadn't seen my father in years and had no idea where he was, I figured I owed it to my son, daughter, and wife to investigate the family members I did know about. I began to reach out to other people on Facebook with the last name McDaniel who were from the same city as my father. After I began to befriend a number of the McDaniels on Facebook, I started to receive emails inquiring about our potential relation. Then, one day, I got a message and really connected with a guy by the name of Deon. He was also a McDaniel living in North Carolina, and he told me that his father and Charlie were brothers. His father died when he was younger, so he didn't have an opportunity to grow up with his biological father either. In addition to that, we also had other things in common, as well, and started to communicate more rapidly. One day, Deon called and informed me that the McDaniel family was having an upcoming reunion that I should attend. It would allow me to meet family members I had never seen or heard of, and for this, I was kind of happy. Finally, I'd get some answers surrounding who I was and where I came from!

After contemplating the decision to go to the family reunion, I had major reservations. I started to think about the fact that I haven't even had a conversation with Charlie McDaniel. At this point, if Charlie McDaniel walked into the room, I wouldn't be able to recognize him. I don't even know if he claims me as his son! After sharing these reservations with Deon, he encouraged me to still come, but he suggested I speak with my father's sister, Aunt Shirley. He felt like she would be able to persuade me to come and everything would be fine.

A few days later, I did speak to Aunt Shirley. I asked her what she remembered about my birth and the history of my mother and her brother's relationship. She confirmed that she remembered my birth and even my father bringing me around. She also confirmed that after a few years, Charlie moved away, and a few years later, he came back and they never heard anything about me anymore. Then she immediately went into the fact that everyone from the family was eager to meet me, my wife, and kids, and we should come to the family reunion. She ended the conversation by saying that even Charlie McDaniel was going to be there. I requested that she call Charlie and arrange a potential meeting between him and I so I could ask questions about the past, get that out of the way, and then attend the family reunion and move on with life. She agreed to call him and contact me the next day.

I never heard from Aunt Shirley again.

After Deon reached out to me again a few weeks later, asking about my attendance at the family reunion, I decided to call and ask my mother her thoughts on the situation and tell her about what happened with Aunt Shirley.

I was quite sensitive not to ask her too many questions about my father because she was going through cancer treatment and had enough stress with the radiation treatments she was now receiving after the surgery she had received months earlier.

I distinctly remember calling her to inquire about the situation, and surprisingly, she welcomed the conversation.

"Momma, what do you think about me reaching out to my dad and his family to potentially connect? They're having a family reunion in a few months, and I was thinking about going."

As I anxiously awaited her response, I was calmed by her immediate reply, "I think that's a great idea, Reco! But why did you think of this all of a sudden?"

"Well, Junior was asking about my daddy and why I didn't know where he was and that he wanted to know him and that side of the family. I felt as though I should attempt to reach out and build a relationship for my children so they can know that side of the family," I said.

Again, without hesitation, she agreed that she thought it was a good idea. I continued by telling her about the conversation I had with Aunt Shirley and how uneasy I felt after she never called me back. I then asked her a question that had been on my mind after speaking with Aunt Shirley.

"Momma, is there any possibility that anyone else could be my father besides Charlie McDaniel?" I asked, barely above a whisper.

I was surprised she wasn't offended by the question. She went on to answer in a normal tone of voice, "You know Reco... when you're young, sometimes you make bad decisions...."

Before she could finish, I immediately cut her off, "What did you say? What do you mean when you're

181

young you make bad decisions?" I shouted into the phone because I was caught off guard and totally confused. "So you're telling me that Charlie McDaniel may not be my father? You've NEVER mentioned this before! Are you serious?" I asked aggressively, not meaning to be disrespectful.

"Reco, I didn't say that Charlie McDaniel wasn't your father, I said that sometimes when you're young, you make bad decisions!" she shot back with a bit of aggression of her own.

Cutting her off again, I said, "But you didn't say, NO, you answered with this, that must mean it is TRUE? This must mean that somebody else could be my father besides Charlie McDaniel?"

As her emotions were clearly running high, she exclaimed, "Charlie McDaniel is your father! And that's it! End of conversation!"

At this point, I could hear her begin to sniffle and noticed that this conversation had terribly upset her. With her health concerns, this was the last thing I wanted to do. So I quickly replied, "Momma, I'm sorry for getting upset and yelling. I didn't mean it. This just caught me off guard. You know what? Forget we even had this conversation. I love you, and I'll talk to you later."

"Okay, I forgive you. I love you, too," she said as the sniffles went away.

As we ended the conversation and hung up the phone, my reservations grew even deeper. The only person I knew to call about this situation was Granny. If anyone knew anything about this, it was her.

So, after hanging up the phone with my mother, I called Granny. I told her the whole story about my conversation with Reco Jr., how I met Deon, the conversation with Aunt Shirley, and finally, about the conversation I had just had minutes earlier with Momma. As I continued questioning Granny about my father, she suddenly grew silent, and then I started to hear her start to sniffle. Granny was crying! I knew then something was up. So I asked, "Granny, is there a possibility that someone else could be my father other than Charlie McDaniel?"

As she cleared her throat and gathered her words, she responded, "Yes, there's a possibility your biological father could be someone else."

I was floored.

When she uttered those words, my life changed forever. How could this be? Is it really true? Is this why I have this nagging feeling in my gut that something's not right? How could Momma keep this possibility from me all my life?

Granny went on to explain that my mother and father had an on-again/off-again relationship when they went to college. Since they were in two different cities and were young, they may have gone out with someone else while they were not seeing each other. In the midst of this, my mother got pregnant.

I guess this is what Momma was referring to when she said, "When you're young, sometimes you make bad decisions."

As Granny continued to explain what happened more than 30 years ago, she described the

184

conversation she had with my mother when my mother told her that she was pregnant. Obviously, my grandmother was disappointed in her because my mother had just enrolled to go to school and was living in Atlanta with Granny's sister and her husband, my mother's uncle and aunt.

Granny then went on to recall and replay the conversation she had with my mother when she found out:

"Deborah, do you know who the father is?" Granny recalled asking my mother.

"Momma, it could be Charlie or this guy I was dating named Chris. Charlie and I had broken up again, and I met Chris. We went out on a few dates and you know... it happened. A few weeks past after that, and I never could get in contact with Chris anymore. That's when me and Charlie got back together," Granny remembered my mother hesitantly explaining to her.

"Well, Deborah, we're not going to play a guessing game! We are going to decide at this moment who the father is. After we decide who the father is, we will never have this conversation again."

After sitting there awhile, Granny said she remembered my mother looking at her and saying with tears running down her face, "I don't know where Chris is, so I believe the father is Charlie."

At that moment, the decision was made that Charlie McDaniel was my father and no one, including Granny or Momma, had brought it up again until this conversation I was having with Granny 30 years later.

After being speechless for a few minutes, at least, I asked Granny who would know about this "Chris" guy. Granny explained that none of my mother's siblings knew about Chris, and neither did anybody else in the family, except for the uncle and aunt my mother was living with at the time she was in college and seeing Chris. This was Uncle Chip and Auntie Emma. I had seen Auntie Emma the year before at a family function, but she had divorced Uncle Chip several years ago. Granny agreed that if I wanted to know more, she would call Auntie Emma and get some information. We agreed to keep this secret from my mother so it wouldn't upset her. I needed to know this information.

Only a day had passed when I got a call from Granny explaining that Uncle Chip would be the one I would have to contact to find out information about Chris. Auntie Emma told her that Chris and Chip were the best of friends during the time my mother and him were going out. But Auntie Emma no longer communicated with Uncle Chip since they had divorced years ago, so I would have to find a way to reach out to him. That's when I decided to turn to the most popular social networking site, Facebook. I ended up finding him because I was a mutual friend with his two sons, my cousins.

After Uncle Chip accepted my friend request via Facebook, we connected over the phone a few times to catch up on old times because it had been more than 15 years since we had seen one another. Because both of us play golf, we were supposed to schedule a tee time and play together, but our schedules never worked out. Finally, after about a month, I couldn't take it anymore, and I called him to let him know the real reason why I searched and found him on Facebook. After going through a similar story that I gave Granny and explaining to him Granny's story, he grew silent. After his silence broke, he responded,

"Reco, to be honest, I didn't recognize your name when I received the friend request over Facebook. But when I looked at your Facebook profile picture, your name didn't come to mind. When I saw your Facebook profile picture, I thought you were my boy Chris from back in the day! I mean, you look exactly like he did when he was 30 years old!"

This was another one of those speechless moments.

After gathering my thoughts, I started to ask questions about who Chris was.

"Do you know what kind of person he is? What does he do for a living? Do you know where he lives? Do you know if he has a wife and children?"

I had so many questions and was eager to find out if this was really a true possibility!

Uncle Chip went on to explain that he hadn't seen Chris in more than 8 years, and he was now living in Georgia. He also stated that before my mother got pregnant with me, Chris had moved to New York and didn't return until years later. Uncle Chip said he didn't think that my mother was pregnant with Chris's child because Chris had been gone for a while by the time everyone knew my mother was pregnant. He just assumed that Charlie was the father. But after seeing my recent pictures and videos online through websites and various speaking engagements, he said he felt certain that Chris was my father.

The emotions surrounding this event were indescribable. Here I am, living the majority of my life possibly hating a man that I didn't even know existed, and it was very possible that he didn't know I existed. I wanted to find out the facts. But I didn't want my mother to find out that I knew. I felt she would think that I would get angry or disappointed, and that's the last thing she would want to happen as this deadly disease begin to take a toll on her. So, I decided to keep this secret while she continued her fight with cancer. The only people that knew about this besides me were Granny, Shanee', Uncle Chip, two of my best friends, and God. In the meantime, I decided to start secretly investigating the situation on my own so I could have all of the information.

After more investigation, I found out that Chris lived in Georgia, was a pastor of a church, and was also a former entrepreneur. I learned that he had a son who was younger than me but looked a lot like my son at the age he was in the pictures I saw. It started to get really ironic when I realized that the home address listed for him was a home that was a short distance from where I lived at the time. If this information was correct, we had lived within one mile from each other for the last 8 years! I was shocked— all this time, my prospective biological father was in driving distance from me and I never knew it up until this point. As I continued to find out all of this information, I couldn't find any pictures of him. Uncle Chip didn't have any, and he didn't know anyone that had any pictures either. I went back to the source that helped me start my investigation: Facebook. Chris didn't have a personal Facebook page, but one of the members of his church had set up a Facebook page for the church.

As I selected the link "Greater Jehovah Baptist Church – Grantville, GA," it seemed like an eternity as the website began to load. I was sure to see this person I had been investigating the last few days. As I started to go through the photo albums on the church's Facebook page, every click to the next photo made me more nervous than the first. This whole situation just seemed like it was out of a dream. As I continued to go through the pictures, I came across a picture that immediately got my attention.

Oh my God! I thought to myself.

I was looking at a picture that had a caption that read, "Pastor Christopher McCambry," and the man in the picture looked like an older version of me!

I must have just sat there for 15 or 20 minutes just staring at the screen. And at this moment, I really didn't know how to feel. After I saved a few of the pictures I found of him on the site, I decided to stop any further investigations and focus on my mother. I didn't want it to continue to consume me and my time if I weren't going to pursue anything at this point.

Time went on, and my focus was back on my mother and her health. Since 2010, I had taken time off from work by ceasing all my speaking engagements, business presentations, and trainings to stay close to my mother's side as she battled this life-threatening disease. As we spent time together during her treatments of chemotherapy and radiation and the many consultations with different doctors, it was always in the back of my mind the secret I was withholding from her.

However, whether or not I told her or kept this all a secret, my mother succumbed to cancer. She lost her battle on July 31, 2011. I was devastated. The one woman who kept me grounded and stable was gone. For the first couple of days, it seemed like I was numb to everything that was going on around me. I was here physically, but my mind was somewhere else. My mother was my world, and I felt like I would be lost without her love and understanding overflowing in my life. Thank God for my family, who was there for me and allowed me to grieve and mourn in my own way. I'm sure some of you who are reading my words right now may know what it's like to lose your mother or father. There is nothing like having to say goodbye to the one responsible for raising you forever. I am just grateful to God that he allowed me to spend so much time with her before she passed away. The financial and time freedom that he allowed me to gain through my entrepreneurial endeavors in network marketing allowed me to be right by her side and not worry about paying my bills in the absence of not working. All of the hard work, dedication, independence, determination, tenacity, and the "never quit" attitude that I gained by watching my mother over the years allowed me to spend almost every day of her last months of life with her. With my wife's support, we even decided to move our family closer to Momma so she could spend more time with us and the kids in the time she had left. All I know is, even though I would give anything to have her back, I keep my eyes and mind focused on the fact that God allowed one of his strongest angels to be on earth with me for 30 years and raise me to become the man I am today.

I am most grateful for that.

I am comforted by the fact that she remains with me in spirit, but at that point, I was faced with the reality that she was gone physically and with her, the identity of my biological father.

A few weeks had passed, and I was still battling with the depression brought on by my mother's death.

Perhaps it was the Holy Spirit that led me, but for some reason, I began my search for Chris again, but this time more aggressively. I was determined to find out who he was and finally figure out if he was the man that gave me life.

After picking up my investigation where I left off, I found the address of his church and also where he was employed. I made a decision, rather than call or email, I would just approach him somehow face-to-face. When he saw me, it's no doubt that he, too, would have some questions. So, after talking with Shanee' and a couple of my best friends, I decided it would be better to show up at his place of employment around the time he got off work. Because of the resemblance, I didn't want to just show up at his church during service. His members would probably have some questions.

On August 31, 2011, exactly 1 month after my mother passed away, I made up my mind that this was the day I would meet Chris. Either way, after today, I would get some answers. After a series of prayers, putting on my clothes, and rehearsing what I was going to say in the mirror, I jumped in the Hummer to drive to Atlanta where Chris worked. It seemed as though everything was trying to delay my arrival. Traffic was horrible trying to make it to that side of town. What would normally be a 30-minute drive ended up being close to an hour and 30 minutes. However anxious, I was still determined to get there. Finally, I did arrive at the building, where I pulled into the parking deck. It took me around 10 to 15 minutes to find somewhere to park.

The anxiety started to grow stronger.

After I parked, I continued to replay in my head what I was going to say upon seeing this guy face-to-face. Then it suddenly hit me like a ton of bricks!

What if I get in here and he's not open at all to what I'm saying?

What if he totally rejects the idea of this being a possibility and tells me to leave the premises?

All of a sudden, I started to rethink my decision and almost went back to my SUV and went home. But at that moment, even though my mother died without knowing what I knew, I felt as though her strength led me to continue into the building and do what I had planned on doing in the first place... confronting Chris about the possibility of him being my biological father.

After around 30 minutes of contemplating and practicing my approach, I walked into the office building. As I walked around the corner nervously, I looked to my right and saw a sign that pointed me in the direction of his suite number. As I approached the suite, I could feel my heart beating in my throat; my palms were sweating, and my legs felt weak. As I approached the front desk, there was a receptionist waiting with a smile.

I know she had to see the amount of distress on my face, but wanting to get this over with as quickly as possible, I asked quickly, "Is Christopher McCambry available?"

Looking rather puzzled, like she could see a physical resemblance between us, she replied, "You just missed him. He just walked out about 3 minutes ago."

I felt like passing out!

I stood there for a few seconds not really knowing what to do next, and then she asked, "Do you have his cell phone number? If not, it's on the bulletin board right outside the door. You can call him."

"Thank you." I said, as I entered the number in my cell phone while my hands were shaking and sweating.

As I made my way back out of the building, I started to think about my next move.

I couldn't let the day pass by without speaking to him. I had worked up to this moment, and I didn't think I could wait another day. I had to talk to him today!

So, I called the cell phone number.

As the phone rang, with every millisecond that passed, it seemed as though my heart was beating faster and faster. And then, finally he answered.

"Hello, this is Chris," a deep voice said on the other end.

"Hey, Chris, my name is Reco. You may not know me, but you actually were involved with my mother several years ago. Her name is Deborah. Does that name ring a bell?" I said, surprised I could get all of that out.

"Deborah, Deborah... Deborah, what's her last name?" he asked.

"Deborah Watson. It was about 31 years ago," I added.

"No, I can't say that I do remember that name. What's going on?" he asked seemingly confused.

"Well, Chris, unfortunately, my mother passed away 1 month ago, but before she passed away, it was brought to my attention that it was a pretty good possibility that you could be my father. So, I wanted to contact you personally and let you know what I know, check it against what you remember, if anything, and decide where we would go from there."

Chapter 14 – The Day Everything Changes

There was complete silence for what seemed like an eternity, but actually, it was only about 5 or 6 seconds. Then he replied, "Wow! You don't get calls like this every day!" as he kind of chuckled, speaking with a crack in his voice. "Well... What did you say your mother's name was again? How old are you, and where are you from?" he asked.

"Her name is Deborah Watson, I am 30 years old, and I am from this area," I responded.

"No, I'm sorry. I don't remember a Deborah Watson. BUT, if you're 30 and I'm 49, that means, if there was a possibility here, I had to be around 18 or 19 when I met your mother. I am also from this area, and I do know I was having sex at that age. Between the ages of 18 and 19, I had visited a cousin in New York for a short weekend getaway. That weekend trip ended up turning into 10 years," he said, as it seemed as though some things were coming together in his head.

When he made that last statement, everything started to come together for me. Granny said that Momma had told her she didn't know where Chris was. Uncle Chip told me that he didn't think Chris knew about me. Maybe there was a real chance that this was it! Maybe this Chris guy was my father!

As these thoughts were rushing through my head, I almost forgot I was on the phone with him. Because he could tell I was nervous, he tried his best to make me feel comfortable.

"So, Reco, what do you do for a living? Is your time flexible? Can you come to my office tomorrow so we can meet up?" he asked.

"Absolutely," I responded.

"Well, my schedule is flexible tomorrow. Any time between 8 a.m. and 4 p.m. works. Just come by so we can discuss this further."

"Ok, well, I guess I'll see you tomorrow. Have a great evening," I said.

After I hung up the phone, it seemed as though I had a huge burden lifted off my shoulders. It seemed as though all of the anxiety I felt up to this point had been taken away. But the meeting was still to come.

That night, I didn't really sleep at all. I was excited yet anxious to meet him for the first time. I continued to tell myself I wasn't going to go into this believing that Chris was my biological father because, after all, there was still a possibly that he wasn't.

So, after making the journey again to his office building, which was a little north of downtown Atlanta, I was calmer and just ready to get this behind me.

As I approached his office suite, following the same path I took the day before, I noticed that it seemed like everything started to happen in slow motion. I noticed this time that the receptionist wasn't at the front desk today. It was a man. This man was on the phone, and ironically, the shape of his head was a lot like mine.

When I had made it to the desk, the man on the phone hung up and looked up at me, and the first thing that came out of his mouth was, "My God, my God...."

After we stood there for a few seconds and he let me into the office, we shook hands looking eye to eye—me standing 6'1" tall and 185lbs, and him standing 6'1" tall and around 175lbs. As we walked over to his desk, it was almost like he was looking at a ghost. I'm sure I was probably looking at him the same way, but I couldn't tell you what expression was on my face. As we started the conversation, I went into more detail about how I had arrived at this point and questioned him about his friendship with my Uncle Chip years ago. As we continued to talk, it seemed like the possibility started to become more of a reality.

After I finished detailing all of the story that had gotten me there, I pulled out my iPad that I had brought in to show him a tribute video I made for my mother that I played during her memorial service less than 30 days before our meeting. The reason why I did this was because there were a number of pictures of my mother in this video from her younger years up until a few years before her sickness.

Not even 5 seconds into the video of the pictures, he said, "Yep, I remember exactly who that is."

He then went on to talk about how although he didn't remember her name, he did remember what a good girl she was. He was a city boy, and my mother was a country girl trying to live in the city when they met. He confirmed that he met her when visiting Uncle Chip one day because she was living with them at the time. They started to go out on a few dates. After they got pretty close, they had sex once, and shortly after that, he went to New York for a weekend trip and stayed for 10 years.

He never knew my mother was pregnant.

In fact, after he left and went to New York, they never spoke again.

After he explained his story and knowing what I knew, everything made perfect sense. We continued to talk in his office for almost 4 hours. It seemed as though we had known each other for a long time. We also started to find out about how much we had in common.

As the clock neared the time for rush hour traffic to begin in Atlanta, I wanted to make sure I left so I wouldn't get caught up in it. I explained to Chris that my family was unaware of the extensive research that I had done and were very protective of me and my mother's image. I said I thought it would be appropriate for us to take a DNA paternity test to have proof that he really was my biological father before we moved forward. Also, it would be great for him and me to know for sure, as well.

His response surprised me, "Reco, I'm totally fine with taking a DNA test if you want one, but after meeting you, I know that you are my son!"

After hearing that statement, I had to hold back tears because I didn't expect this to happen like this, especially so quickly. But I welcomed his openness and told him for the sake of both our families, I thought this would be the right thing to do.

Although it took a few days to get the test results back, Chris and I started to talk each day while we waited for them to come back in. Any hesitations I had about this man were quickly dismissed once I learned the type of man he was, the morals he held, and how willing he was to accept me into his family and his church. A little more than a week from the day we met, we got the results back from the lab, and it was confirmed—Chris McCambry was my biological father.

I never thought I would be happy to know that I actually had a father, but I was thankful to God that this man was mine. Even though we had a lot to learn about one another, I had faith that it was going to be a great experience. One of the happiest moments of my life after I received the results was getting Reco Jr. on the phone with him and introducing him to his "Granddaddy," something that may never have happened if he hadn't had that conversation with me that day in December of 2009.

When Reco Jr. and Chris met for the first time, it was like something out of a movie when they hugged; it made me shed a few tears.

It really made me realize that all of this was actually worth it, and I had a responsibility to get rid of the anger and resentment for the health of my family.

After a few months of communicating and meeting up, I asked Chris if it was ok for me to call him Dad. He never pressed that point, but he was honored by the fact I would ask. To date, I have been met with plenty of love and support from him and his family, now my family, and one that I had missed out on my entire life. I remember the moment he introduced me to his church as his son: It's a memory I will never forget. Yes, it was a lot to take in in a short period of time; however, my heart is filled with the love they sent my way (and continue to send my way) on a daily basis.

Presently, my father, his family, and my family get together as often as possible. He is one of my best friends and closest confidants. We are so much alike! We both were young fathers who went on to create a successful business and gain the admiration from family and the general public. We are both testaments proving that life doesn't always go the way you plan it to go, but that doesn't mean you can't strive for the best and move ahead.

This story is an important one for you to digest and apply to your own life. Everything wasn't what it seemed to be. For 30 years, I believed a truth that wasn't the actual reality. However, I chose to accept it and make the best of it, something I encourage each of you to do. Life has a way of throwing curve balls at you. It will sometimes move you off balance and spring a surprise on you when you least expect it. My advice to you? **Make the best of it. Accept the new challenge. Don't let it make you angry or resentful**. I spent too much of my life being consumed by conflicting emotions surrounding being fatherless and feeling alone. Now that I have my real dad in my life, I will thank God for His blessing and make up for the time I've missed being a son to a man who wants me in his life.

The Fatherless Father

Chapter 15 – The First Day of the Rest of Your Life

"Go confidently in the direction of your dreams. Live the life you have imagined."
–Henry David Thoreau, author

There has been a great deal of material covered in this book and a lot of food for thought that you'll need to digest. However, if you leave with nothing else, remember this: NOW is the time for you to make critically smart decisions that will lead to the defining moments in your life. Everything that you have accomplished this year, this month, this day, and this moment is only a fraction of what is *truly* possible for you.

We all have a champion inside of us that is waiting to come out, we just have to be willing enough to reach deep inside of ourselves and bring that potential to the surface. People like Michael Jordan, Oprah

Winfrey, Barack Obama, Steve Jobs, and Martin
Luther King, Jr. all realized they had potential to do
great things; they just needed to maintain their faith,
stay on course towards their dreams, and find their
inner champion.

As you've gathered from the previous chapters, I
had to find my inner champion over the course of my
lifetime. I can tell you right now, IT WAS NOT EASY.
Words on pages cannot truly convey the amount of
blood, sweat, and tears I've had to put in to get to
where I am today. However, I wouldn't trade those
moments for the world because they actually helped
me become the man I am today. My past has taught
me a number of valuable lessons.

1. **Everything is not what it seems.**
   My discovery of my biological father
   completely changed my life. Had it not
   been for me asking questions and
   reaching out to certain people, my
   father's identity would still remain a
   mystery. This discovery taught me to
   always be open to change, even if that
   change is something that's life-

changing. Author William Arthur Ward said it best, "The pessimist complains about the wind; the optimist expects it to change; the realist adjusts the sails."

2. **Only you know how much you're willing to invest.** Some people call it sacrifice. But in my opinion, there is a difference between sacrificing and investing. When you sacrifice something, you can never get it back. But when you invest something, the expectation is to get it back plus much more! I graduated top of my class in high school. When I was 18, I started working for a major energy company in Georgia. By the time I was 23, I had my first custom home built. In my mid-20s, I had built a business producing millions of dollars in revenue. And at the age of 30, I started running my own companies. ALL of these things were accomplished because I invested my faith, time, energy, focus, efforts, and money to

reap multiple rewards now. Look at your present challenges as if they are investing in a better future for you, not taking away from your present. You will last in the fight longer that way. Former United States President Theodore Roosevelt once said, "Nothing in the world is worth having or worth doing unless it means effort, pain, and difficulty... I have never in my life envied a human being who led an easy life. I have envied a great many people who led difficult lives and led them well." Momma always told me something that I live by every day, and you should, too. She said, "If it's worth having, it's worth fighting for." People will respect you more for it, and you will realize the power you have over your own life.

3. **Don't let a setback set *you* back.** I could have used growing up in a single-parent household as an excuse. I could have let the unexpected news that I'd be a father at 19 years old

deter me from my goals. However, I chose to push forward and hustle harder. This is what I encourage all of you to do—push harder. It's so much easier to give up than to keep going. Make the choice to keep your eyes on the prize and don't look back. Advice columnist Ann Landers wrote, "Nobody gets to live life backwards. Look ahead. That is where your future lies." Again, a setback should not determine the way you live your life. Always remember, where you are does not define who you are. Who you are is defined by where you're going and what you believe!

4. **Don't be afraid to ask for help.** When I found out my college girlfriend was pregnant with my son, I reached out to Auntie Paulette and asked for her advice and assistance. When I had questions about the identity of my biological father, I reached out to various family members, including my grandmother and my uncle, to figure

out who that man could be. No one gets to be successful in life without the help and assistance of someone else. Some people look at asking for assistance as a weakness. However, I recognize it as something that made my life easier; this same rule goes for you. "Those who are happiest are those who do the most for others," said inventor Booker T. Washington. Asking for help and giving help is a basic human need. Embrace that.

5. **Let go of negative emotions.** Finally, I want to make certain that everyone must understand that much of the reason why we can't break through most of life's barriers is because many times we are that barrier. We let negative thoughts and emotions control our lives, and we are forced to live below our true potential. I lived with secret anger and resentment for years as a child, teenager, and into my 20s. When I was able to let those emotions go, I

was much more productive and, eventually, found myself open to finding out the truth, leading me to finding and building a relationship with my biological father.

In closing, I want to address a question that I'm frequently asked when people hear my story, which is about my mother keeping this information from me my entire life and me not having the opportunity to have my father in my life. People ask me, "Reco, were you upset with your mother when you found out that she had kept this from you for so many years?"

My answer is always, "Absolutely not."

My mother did the best she could with what she had. Sometimes we didn't have much, but we always had God, and we made it just fine.

She could have certainly told me about the conversation she had with Granny, but honestly, I'm quite happy how my life has turned out, knowing what I knew for the first 30 years of my life. And I feel like I had a better upbringing and turned out just as good as children who had both parents in their home.

So, if you're reading this book right now, and if you are in the unfortunate situation of not having the father of your child there with you for whatever reason, it's okay. You are just as capable of raising a successful child as my mother raised me. Hopefully, the stories and lessons in this book that stemmed from her success are something you can take and add to your own success.

To all my fathers reading this book that grew up fatherless, or if you are a father and you're struggling with the ability to be held accountable and be there for your children, I'm here to tell you, it can be done. There is no greater feeling in the world to know that by your direction and protection, with God's help, your children can grow up and live more healthy and prosperous lives. They are counting on you, and we other fathers are counting on you.

You can do it.

Finally, if you're reading this book and you are fatherless, never forget that our heavenly Father is all you need to see you through. Prior to me meeting my biological father, God saw me through all the trials and tribulations that I was certain would bury me. So, if you are looking for wholeness, happiness, prosperity, a change of mind, courage, strength, or whatever you're looking for, remember that He is all the father you need. I'm not ending this book with a religious sermon, but I am telling you that there was a reason you purchased this book and read it all the way to the end to approach this very moment. Developing a relationship with Him will exceed any help you could get from a book, therapist, motivational speaker, or TV show. This relationship will help you gain the peace of mind you need to succeed at life at the highest level and to possibly, one day, become that fatherless father that will inspire change in millions of lives across the world, as I pray that this book does.

May God bless you, and good luck in all your endeavors.

Reco

What's Next...

Thank you for your support and interest in The Fatherless Father. Reco is very passionate about others being able to overcome adversity and achieve their dreams. It is our goal to reach over 10 million households globally over the next decade affected by this Fatherless epidemic and redirect a generation towards positive change.

If this book has touched your life and you would like to expose others to its message and many lessons, we would like you to join us by doing one or more of the following:

1. Send us a review with your thoughts. Go to www.TheFatherlessFather.com and submit your feelings about the book. This will encourage others to join our mission.

2. Purchase a book from our website for someone you know that could benefit from it and we'll ship it to them.

3. Purchase a book from our website for an anonymous single mother, teenager, or father that will be distributed from one of the organizations we support that deal with this epidemic globally.

4. If you are a Fatherless Father, we would like to hear from you. Tell us your story. Email info@thefatherlessfather.com.

5. Visit www.TheFatherlessFather.com and connect with us on your favorite Social Networks and "share" our page to spread the word about the mission.

The Fatherless Father
2385 Wall Street
Conyers, GA 30013
office: 1.800.995.5251   fax: 678.528.9513
email: info@thefatherlessfather.com
web: www.thefatherlessfather.com

About the Author

Reco McDaniel has been blessed to accomplish a tremendous amount at a young age. Becoming a successful entrepreneur in his 20s, Reco now serves as President and CEO of two Atlanta-based marketing companies, C.O.D.E. R.E.D. Marketing (CRM) and Elite Profit Network (EPN). Coaching and consulting executives and sales teams on a monthly basis, CRM is one of the leading training providers for network marketing business professionals in the southeast. Additionally, through his disciplined financial oversight and business savvy, he helped build EPN's independent sales force nationwide. To date, EPN has established hundreds of strategic partnerships with approximately 600 online distributors to deliver quality products and services to consumers across the country.

As a talented speaker, Reco is frequently tapped by corporations, non-profits, youth programs, faith-based organizations and educational institutions to share the keys of his successful entrepreneurial endeavors. He offers audiences a candid peek into his personal experiences and provides motivation and encouragement to inspire positive life changes and success.

Featured as one of the youngest success stories in the most recent edition of Who's Who in Black Atlanta", Reco is an active member of the National Speakers Association, both national and local chapters, and The Global Speakers Federation. He currently fulfills numerous speaking engagements across the country, transcending cultural and socioeconomic barriers with his messages on personal growth, spiritual fulfillment and financial stability.

As a leader and problem-solver, Reco is also committed to taking tremendous strides to impact his local community. In 2008, he founded a Youth Mentorship Program, a pro bono mentorship program for Atlanta's youth and young professionals. In addition to the Youth Mentorship Program, Reco also launched The Elite Cause in 2009. This program annually adopts 12 low-income families to provide resources – from food to gifts to other assistance – to ensure they receive the loving support needed at that time.

Reco currently resides in Atlanta with his wife Shanee', son Reco Jr. and daughter Raegan. He is motivated by the teaching that "We are blessed by God to be a blessing to others", and credits his success to his faith in God and obligation to his family.

For more information on Reco McDaniel, visit www.RecoMcDaniel.com.